THE

1619

PROJECT

A CRITIQUE

PHILLIP W. MAGNESS

AMERICAN INSTITUTE FOR ECONOMIC RESEARCH

By Phillip W. Magness

ISBN: 9781630692018

Cover art: Vanessa Mendozzi

THE

1619

PROJECT

A CRITIQUE

PHILLIP W. MAGNESS

AIER | AMERICAN INSTITUTE
for ECONOMIC RESEARCH

Contents

Preface

When I first weighed in upon the *New York Times*' 1619 Project, I was struck by its conflicted messaging. Comprising an entire magazine feature and a sizable advertising budget, the newspaper's initiative conveyed a serious attempt to engage the public in an intellectual exchange about the history of slavery in the United States and its lingering harms to our social fabric. It also seemed to avoid the superficiality of many public history initiatives, which all too often reduce over 400 complex years of slavery's history and legacy to sweeping generalizations. Instead, the *Times* promised detailed thematic explorations of topics ranging from the first slave ship's arrival in Jamestown, Virginia, in 1619 to the politics of race in the present day.

At the same time, however, certain 1619 Project essayists infused this worthy line of inquiry with a heavy stream of ideological advocacy. *Times* reporter Nikole Hannah-Jones announced this political intention openly, pairing progressive activism with the initiative's stated educational purposes.

Signs of the blurred lines between scholarship and activism appeared in several, though not all, of its essays. A historical discussion about the Constitution's notoriously strained handling of slavery quickly drifted into a list of partisan grievances against the tax and health care policy views of congressional Republicans in the twenty-first century. Another potentially interesting inquiry into the history of how city planning historically intertwined with racial segregation ended with a harangue against suburban Atlanta voters for declining to fund an expensive and ineffectual light-rail transit project at the ballot box. Hannah-Jones's own introductory essay presented a provocative conceptual reframing of American history around slavery, hence 1619 rather than 1776 as its titular origin date, albeit with an almost-singular mind toward advocating for a slavery-reparations program in the present.

Enlisting history for political editorializing is a time-honored habit of commentators across the political spectrum, so in a sense the 1619 Project's indulgences in the same were unexceptional. The *Times'* branding, however, exhibited a schizophrenia of purposes.

Hannah-Jones's own public comments pivoted between touting her work as the culmination of rigorous historical scholarship and an exercise in advocacy journalism—seemingly as the occasion demanded. The 1619 Project, it seemed, could serve as both an enduring long-term curriculum for high school and college classrooms and an activist manual for the 2020 campaign season. Unfortunately the blending of these two competing aims usually results in the sacrifice of scholarly standards in the service of the ideological objective—not by design, but by necessary implication of needing to reconcile the irreducible complexities of the past to a more simplistic political narrative.

This tendency finds its most visible display in the 1619 Project contribution that first caught my attention, Matthew Desmond's essay on the relationship between slavery and modern American capitalism. Having explored this topic extensively in my own scholarly work on economic and intellectual history, I was immediately struck by the shallow one-sidedness of Desmond's argument.

Among economic historians, few subjects are more heavily scrutinized than the operations of the antebellum slave economy. The existent literature dates back half a century and encompasses hundreds of works from across the ideological spectrum, each employing empirical data to better understand the profitability, efficiency, and state sanction of the plantation system. Curiously, Desmond's article evinced no awareness of the scholarly study of slavery beyond a narrow coterie of post-2010 historical works going by the moniker of the "New History of Capitalism" (NHC).

Although it has yielded modestly interesting archival insights about plantation operations, the NHC school of slavery scholarship also suffers from a notorious ideological and methodological insularity—the subject of a 2017 historiographical essay that I wrote for another book and that is adapted for the present volume. As that chapter documents, two defining characteristics of the NHC literature are (1) its recurring, and at times even inept, misuse of economic data to make unsupported empirical claims, and (2) its heavily anticapitalist political perspective. While both attributes have earned the NHC severe criticism among historians and economic historians of slavery from outside its ranks, the group has thus far taken few steps to reconcile its shortcomings with a broader scholarly literature that often belies the main NHC contentions. It therefore came as a surprise to find that Desmond had relied almost exclusively on contested claims from the NHC literature to build his argument, albeit without any hint of the associated contestation.

To this end, he casually repeated an erroneous NHC claim about the cause of cotton productivity growth in the early nineteenth century and further misrepresented its historical evidence to suggest an unsupported origin story for modern business practices in the accounting books of nineteenth-century plantations. The resulting argument advanced a specious link between slavery in the nineteenth century and capitalism today. Lurking beneath it all was a long list of Desmond's own modern progressive political causes—economic inequality, financial reforms after the 2007–8 financial crisis, and a general disdain for deregulation and free market thought. In short, Desmond was weaponizing the history of slavery to attack modern capitalism.

I entered the fray of the 1619 Project debate in its first week, with a series of articles scrutinizing Desmond's narrative and contextualizing them within what Friedrich A. Hayek dubbed the "anti-capitalist" tradition in intellectual life. From there I joined a broader discussion involving dozens of historians, economists, and other scholars that began to scrutinize other historical claims in the project, particularly Hannah-Jones's attempts to recast the American Revolution as being primarily motivated by the preservation of slavery.

Not all 1619 Project criticisms hit their mark though, and in the course of the ensuing months I broke from several of the other historian critics over the *Times'* depiction of Abraham Lincoln. Hannah-Jones pointed out the sixteenth president's recurring interest in colonizing freed slaves abroad after emancipating them, mainly to call attention to Lincoln's complex and sometimes neglected beliefs about race in a post-slavery society. This earned her the animosity of a group of historian critics on both the political left and right, including accusations of unfairly disparaging Lincoln. Having devoted a significant amount of my own scholarly work to Lincoln's presidency, I weighed in on the arguments as presented, showing that the 1619 Project's assessment was in closer line with historical evidence that these critics neglected to consider. The essays are presented herein, and they place me in the curious position of being one of the only 1619 Project critics to also come to its defense on one of the major points of contention.

In assembling these essays, I make no claim of resolving what continues to be a vibrant and ongoing discussion. Neither should my work be viewed as the final arbiter of historical accuracy, though I do evaluate a number of factual and interpretive claims made by the project's authors. Rather, the aim is to provide an accessible resource for readers wishing to navigate the scholarly disputes, offering my own interpretive take on claims pertaining to areas of history in which I have worked.

Phillip W. Magness
March 2020

How the 1619 Project Rehabilitates the 'King Cotton' Thesis

This essay, originally written for National Review, *examines the 1619 Project's heavy reliance on the New History of Capitalism (NHC) literature. A recurring theme of this literature is the unwitting rehabilitation of the "King Cotton" thesis—the notion that cotton occupied a commanding place in the 19th century global economy, and as such the economic engines of the world were claimed to depend on plantation slavery. Confederate secessionists invented "King Cotton" as part of a proslavery propaganda campaign around the eve of the Civil War as an attempt to lure foreign allies to their cause.*

The war itself disproved the "King Cotton" premise, as foreign powers simply turned elsewhere for their cotton supply and the Confederacy collapsed in economic isolation from the world. While most economic historians since that time have recognized the error of logic behind the "King Cotton" theory, the recent NHC literature has

revived it—minus the Confederates' slavery defenses—in an
attempt to restore cotton to a historically untenable place
as the centerpiece of 19ᵗʰ century capitalism.

* * *

'I say that cotton is king, and that he waves his scepter not only over these 33 states, but over the island of Great Britain and over continental Europe!" So thundered Senator Louis T. Wigfall of Texas in December 1860, as an intended warning to those who doubted the economic viability of secessionism. Like many Southerners, Wigfall subscribed to the "King Cotton" thesis: the belief that slave-produced cotton commanded a controlling position over the American economy and indeed the world's commercial engines. Developed in the 1850s by political economist David Christy and championed by the radical pro-slavery politician James Henry Hammond, that argument was to be the nascent Confederacy's trump card—an engine of global wealth in which all other economic activities were intertwined. Indeed, no nation would dare make war upon plantation slavery, for if the South suspended its production, in the words of Hammond, "we could bring the whole world to our feet."

The strategy failed. The secessionists effectively self-embargoed what remained of their export crop in the wake of the war's physical destruction and the Union's blockade, and attempts to draw the European powers into the war on the Confederacy's behalf were unsuccessful. King Cotton, in practice, proved nothing more than part self-delusion and part racist propaganda to rationalize the supposed economic necessity of chattel slavery. Modern empirical analysis has similarly debunked its claims: As Harvard economist Nathan

Nunn has demonstrated, a strong negative relationship exists between the historical existence of slavery in a county or state and its level of income, persisting to the present day.[1]

Yet despite its historical untenability, the economic reasoning behind "King Cotton" has undergone a surprising—perhaps unwitting—rehabilitation through a modern genre of scholarly works known as the New History of Capitalism (NHC). While NHC historians reject the pro-slavery thrust of Wigfall and Hammond's bluster, they recast slave-produced cotton as "not just as an integral part of American capitalism, but... its very essence," to quote Harvard's Sven Beckert. Cornell historian Ed Baptist goes even further, describing slavery as the indispensable causal driver behind America's wealth today. Cotton production, he contends, was "absolutely necessary" for the Western world to break the "10,000-year Malthusian cycle of agriculture."

And this same NHC literature provides the scholarly foundation of the ballyhooed *New York Times'* 1619 Project—specifically, its foray into the economics of slavery. Guided by this rehabilitated version of King Cotton, Princeton sociologist Matthew Desmond enlists the horrors of the plantation system to launch a blistering attack on modern American capitalism.

Desmond projects slavery's legacy onto a litany of tropes about rising inequality, the decline of labor-union power, environmental destruction, and the 2008 financial crisis. The intended message is clear: modern capitalism carries with it the stain of slavery, and its putative excesses are proof of its continued brutality. It follows that only by

....

1 Nunn, Nathan. 2008. "Slavery, Inequality, and Economic Development in the Americas: An Examination of the Engerman-Sokoloff Hypothesis." *Helpman E Institutions and Economic Performance*, pp. 148-180. Cambridge: Harvard University Press.

abandoning the free market and embracing political redistribution will we ever atone for this tainted inheritance.

It's not just the *New York Times* that uses NHC scholarship to distort the economic history of the U.S. At a congressional hearing earlier this summer, journalist Ta-Nehisi Coates enlisted another of Baptist's claims to argue for reparations. "By 1836 more than $600 million, almost half of the economic activity in the United States, derived directly or indirectly from the cotton produced by the million-odd slaves," Coates said.

This stunning statistic quickly became one of the most memorable sound bites of the occasion. It is also unambiguously false—the result of Baptist double- and triple-counting intermediate transactions from cotton production to artificially increase its economic share.[2] Through an elementary accounting error, Baptist had inflated the actual size of the cotton sector by almost tenfold. At approximately 5 to 6 percent of the antebellum economy, cotton did indeed constitute a major output, roughly comparable in size to the northern-dominated railroad sector. It was not, however, the commercial monarch of either Confederate fantasy or Baptist's revisionism.

Dubious statistical claims and shoddy research practices are alarmingly common in the broader NHC literature. Those who rely on it repeat these mistakes. In the 1619 Project, Desmond uses another of Baptist's statistics to attribute a 400 percent increase in the daily yield of cotton-picking between 1800 and 1860 to the systematization of whipping and torture as a means of increasing production. This "calibrated torture" thesis forms the central claim of Baptist's 2014 book, *The Half Has Never Been Told*, purporting to show that

....

2 See chapter herein entitled "The Statistical Errors of the Reparations Agenda."

slave-based production was a capitalistic enterprise at its core. Furthermore, Baptist claims that modern industrial-management techniques (the recording of daily outputs, the comparative tracking of employee productivity, the keeping of double-entry accounting books) take a page from the most evil chapter of American history.

Yet again, Baptist's thesis is built on misinterpreted evidence—or perhaps intentional deception. He bases his argument on the empirical work of economists Alan Olmstead and Paul Rhode, who assembled decades of plantation records to study the growth in cotton-crop yields before the Civil War. Olmstead and Rhode discovered the same 400 percent increase in cotton-picking rates yet found a completely different cause: yields grew primarily as a result of technological improvements to the crop from cross-breeding different strains of cotton seed.

Olmstead and Rhode published a stinging rebuke of Baptist's work, showing empirically that cotton-picking yields tended to follow daily variations across the crop season, not Baptist's posited use of a torture-enforced quota system.[3] In addition to his faulty GDP statistics, they showed that Baptist severely overstated the amount of wealth tied up in slavery. "The upshot," they note, "is that slaves represented an important share of U.S. wealth but not nearly as great as Baptist claimed."

They also uncovered evidence of Baptist massaging the details of primary-source accounts such as slave narratives to bolster his thesis. This included adding words to slave testimonies and blending passages from disparate sources to change their meaning. These suspicious edits make accounts of the treatment of slaves appear more similar to

....

3 Olmstead, Alan L. and Paul W. Rhode. 2018. "Cotton, slavery, and the new history of capitalism." *Explorations in Economic History*, January.

modern-day managerial tactics.

The economists do not contest or downplay the violent reality of plantation life, acknowledging openly that the widespread "use of violence or the threat of violence increased slave output." But they document several instances of Baptist playing fast and loose with the evidence, either to exaggerate the resemblance of chattel slavery to modern managerial practices or to inflate the size of the plantation system and treat it as the single dominant economic force in antebellum America.

Curiously, participants of the 1619 Project evince little awareness of the deep historical deficiencies in Baptist's work or of similar problems among the other NHC scholars on whom they rest their case. When I asked Nikole Hannah-Jones, the project's editor, about its repetition of erroneous and contested economic claims, she said, "Economists dispute a few of Baptist's calculations but not the book itself nor its thesis."[4]

Really? Contrast that with Olmstead's concluding assessment: "Edward Baptist's study of capitalism and slavery is flawed beyond repair."[5] Or Wellesley economist Eric Hilt's review essay, in which he identifies "specious arguments and failures of analytical reasoning" in the NHC literature and chastises the genre for the way its "neglect of insights from economic history often weakens its analysis and undermines its credibility as social criticism."[6] Or the observation

....

4 Hannah-Jones, Nikole. 2019. "Economists dispute a few of Baptist's calculations but not the book itself nor its thesis." Twitter, August 18, 2019. https://twitter.com/nhannahjones/status/1163030801778401281

5 Murray, J., Olmstead, A., Logan, T., Pritchett, J., & Rousseau, P. 2015. "Roundtable of Reviews for 'The Half Has Never Been Told: Slavery and the Making of American Capitalism' By Edward E. Baptist." *The Journal of Economic History,* 75(03): 919-931.

6 Hilt, Eric. 2017. "Economic History, Historical Analysis, and the "New History of Capitalism"". *The Journal of Economic History*, 77(2): 511-536.

by Stanley Engerman, who in his co-authored work *Time on the Cross* defined the modern field on the economics of slavery, that Baptist does not meaningfully engage with "the last decades of works concerning economic aspects of the slave economy," many of which cut directly against his conclusions.[7] Indeed, much of the self-asserted novelty of the NHC historians seems to reflect their own unfamiliarity with the economic literature on the same subject. And Baptist, to his discredit, has generally declined to answer the substantive criticisms of his work, even as his errors spread to wider audiences via the press.

Like the original "King Cotton" thesis, the NHC suffers from its own ideological disposition. Though one sought to prop up slavery in its own day and the other condemns it historically, both build their evidence by working backward from the preexisting conclusion of its economic vitality. Both then advance the simply false assertion that this economic vitality was the driving engine of the antebellum economy.

The thrust of these exaggerations is to recast slavery as a distinctly capitalistic enterprise, which, in turn, services the 1619 Project's political message. The worthy historical task of documenting the horrors of American slavery has been cynically repurposed into an ideological attack on free-market capitalism. But in a curious final twist, the "King Cotton" theorists of old would have likely balked at the decision by their latter-day inheritors to label plantation slavery a capitalistic enterprise. To the original pro-slavery theorists, the very free-market theories that Baptist and the *New York Times* indict were an existential threat. The philosophical doctrines we now know as

....

7 Engerman, Stanley L. 2017. "Review of 'The Business of Slavery and the Rise of American Capitalism, 1815-1860' by Calvin Schermerhorn and 'The Half Has Never Been Told: Slavery and the Making of American Capitalism' by Edward E. Baptist." *Journal of Economic Literature*, 55(2): 637-43.

capitalism were "tainted with abolition, and at war with our institu-tions," to quote an 1857 tract by leading pro-slavery theorist George Fitzhugh. For slavery to survive this attack, he said, the South must "throw Adam Smith, Say, Ricardo & Co., in the fire."[8]

Insofar as the 1619 Project seeks to teach American society about the horrific historical legacy of slavery, it is no small irony that a significant part of the project borrows from a historical literature that apparently envisions a similar future for Adam Smith's heirs.

....

8 Fitzhugh, George. 1857. *Cannibals All! Or, Slaves Without Masters* (electron-ic ed.). Richmond: A. Morris, Publisher.

The Anti-Capitalist Ideology of Slavery

In this essay, I examine the first of many oversights in Matthew Desmond's 1619 Project essay, in which he asserts that American capitalism is infused with the brutality of the slave system. Briefly, his account completely neglects the role of intellectual history in defining and interpreting capitalism. Upon examining this history, two trends emerge.

First, the originators of what we now refer to as "capitalism"—the free market liberal tradition that passed from Adam Smith to the laissez-faire and free trade traditions of Richard Cobden and Frederic Bastiat—had a directly adversarial view of slavery. Economists and political writers in this tradition heavily overlapped with the contemporary abolitionist movement and tended to view slavery as both morally and economically repulsive.

Second, pro-slavery theorists of this same period also held capitalism in contempt—and especially its laissez-faire iteration. I document this pronounced hostility to capitalism in the work of George Fitzhugh, the leading proslavery theorist of the late antebellum period. For academics such as Desmond

*who wish to forge a conceptual alliance between slavery and
capitalism, this historical record of capitalism's proponents
and adversaries remains a substantial and unaccounted
obstacle.*

* * *

What is capitalism's view toward slavery? It seems like a crazy
question, but not so much actually, not in these times. So let us begin
with the opening line of the first chapter of George Fitzhugh's *Sociology
for the South*, first published in 1854:[9]

> Political economy is the science of free society. Its theory and
> its history alike establish this position. Its fundamental maxim
> Laissez-faire and "Pas trop gouverner," are at war with all kinds
> of slavery, for they in fact assert that individuals and peoples
> prosper most when governed least.

Fitzhugh's point was to inveigh against economic freedom and in
defense of slavery. His radical tract sought to make out an elaborate
ideological case for slave labor and indeed all aspects of social
ordering. Such a system, he announced, would resolve the posited
state of perpetual conflict between labor and the owners of capital by
supplanting it with the paternalistic hierarchy of slavery—a model
he advocated not only for the plantations of the South but also for
adaptation to the factories of the Northeast.

....

9 Fitzhugh, George. 1854. *Sociology for the South Or The Failure of Free Society* (electronic ed.). Richmond: A. Morris, Publisher.

In total, Fitzhugh presented a horrifying vision of a national society reordered around the principle of chattel slavery. And as his introductory remarks announced, attainment of that society required the defeat of its remaining obstacle, the free market.

Although his theories are rightly rejected today, the Virginia-born Fitzhugh attained national prominence in the late antebellum period as one of the most widely read defenders of a slave-based economy. Charles Sumner called him a "leading writer among Slave-masters," and his regular contributions to the pro-South magazine *DeBow's Review* gained him a national readership in the 1850s.

In 1855 Fitzhugh embarked on a publicity tour of the Northeast, jousting with abolitionist Wendell Phillips in a series of back-to-back lectures on the slavery question. By 1861, he had added his voice to the cause of southern secessionism and began mapping out an elaborate slave-based industrialization policy for the Confederacy's wartime economy.[10]

Fitzhugh was also an avowed anti-capitalist. Slavery's greatest threat came from the free market economic doctrines of Europe, which were "tainted with abolition, and at war with our institutions." According to him, the South's survival required "throw[ing] Adam Smith, Say, Ricardo & Co., in the fire."

Such rhetoric presents an under-acknowledged conundrum for modern historians. In contemporary acadamia it has become trendy to depict plantation slavery as an integral component of American capitalism.

A new multipart feature series in the *New York Times* advances this

....

10 Fitzhugh, George. 1861. "The Times and The War." *De Bow's Review*, 31(1), 1-13.

thesis, depicting modern free market capitalism as an inherently "racist" institution and a direct lineal descendant of plantation slavery, still exhibiting the brutality of that system.[11] This characterization draws heavily from the so-called "New History of Capitalism" (NHC)—a genre of historical writing that swept through the academy in the last decade and that aggressively promotes the thesis that free market capitalism and slavery are inextricably linked.

Many leading examples of NHC scholarship in the academy today are plagued by shoddy economic analysis and documented misuse of historical evidence.[12] These works often present historically implausible arguments, such as the notion that modern double-entry accounting emerged from plantation ledger books (the practice actually traces to the banking economies of Renaissance Italy), or that its use by slave owners is distinctively capitalistic (even the Soviets employed modern accounting practices, despite attempting to centrally plan their entire economy). Indeed, it was NHC historian Ed Baptist who produced an unambiguously false statistic purporting to show that cotton production accounted for a full half of the antebellum American economy (when in actual fact it comprised about 5 percent of GDP).[13]

Despite the deep empirical and historical deficiencies of this literature, NHC arguments are still widely enlisted not only as historical analysis of slavery's economics but as an ideological attack on modern

....

11 Desmond, Matthew. 2019. "American Capitalism is Brutal. You Can Trace That to the Plantation." The New York Times Magazine, August 14.

12 Olmstead, Alan L. and Paul W. Rhode. 2018. "Cotton, slavery, and the new history of capitalism." *Explorations in Economic History*, January.

13 See chapter herein entitled "The Statistical Errors of the Reparations Agenda;" Baptist, Edward E. 2014. *The Half Has Never Been Told: Slavery and the Making of American Capitalism*. New York: Basic Books.

capitalism itself. If capitalism is historically tainted by its links to slavery, they reason, then the effects of slavery's stain persist in modern American capitalism today. In its most extreme iterations, these same historians then advocate a political reordering of the American economy to remove that stain. In other words, to reconcile our society to its history and atone for the sins of slavery, we must abandon what remains of American capitalism.

The NHC literature's use of the term "capitalism" is plagued by its own definitional fluidity, which, at times, encompasses everything from laissez-faire non-intervention to protectionist mercantilism to state-ordered central planning. Most economic historians take care to differentiate between the features of these widely varying systems; however, the NHC literature has adopted a habit of simply relabeling everything as "capitalism." A command-and-control wartime industrial policy thus becomes "war capitalism," while a slave-oriented mercantilist regime of protective tariffs and industrial subsidies becomes "racial slave capitalism," and so forth.

When brandished in modern politics, it quickly becomes clear that the same scholars have only one "capitalism" in mind. The NHC genre's own economic inclinations veer unambiguously in a leftward direction, suggesting their real ire is toward the classical liberal free market variety of capitalism. Wealth redistribution, the nationalization of health care and other entire economic sectors, socialistic central planning of industries around labor activism, and even a plethora of climate change policies thereby become necessary acts of "social justice" to correct for capitalism's supposed slavery-infused legacy.

We therefore arrive at the curious position wherein "atonement" for slavery, as presented by the NHC historians, involves politically repudiating the same free market doctrines that Fitzhugh deemed the greatest danger to slavery itself in the decade before the Civil War.

Returning to Fitzhugh's defense of slavery, we find deep similarities to anti-capitalist rhetoric today. The economic doctrines of laissez-faire, he wrote in 1857, foster "a system of unmitigated selfishness."[14] They subject nominally free labor to the "despotism of capital" wherein the capitalist class extracts an "exploitation of skill" from wage laborers, as found in the difference between the value of what they create and the much lower compensation they receive.

As Fitzhugh argued, by way of the example of a wealthy acquaintance who had "ceased work" and lived off of his fortune, the capitalist's "capital was but the accumulation of the results of their labor; for common labor creates all capital." He then succinctly explained the result by noting "the capitalist, living on his income, gives nothing to his subjects. He lives by mere exploitation." As Fitzhugh continued:

> It is the interest of the capitalist and the skillful to allow free laborers the least possible portion of the fruits of their own labor; for all capital is created by labor, and the smaller the allowance of the free laborer, the greater the gains of his employer. To treat free laborers badly and unfairly, is universally inculcated as a moral duty, and the selfishness of man's nature prompts him to the most rigorous performance of this cannibalish duty. We appeal to political economy; the ethical, social, political and economic philosophy of free society, to prove the truth of our doctrines. As an ethical and social guide, that philosophy teaches, that social, individual and national competition, is a moral duty,

....

14 Fitzhugh, George. 1857. *Cannibals All! Or, Slaves Without Masters* (electronic ed.). Richmond: A. Morris, Publisher.

and we have attempted to prove all competition is but the effort to enslave others, without being encumbered with their support.

The difference between the value of the laborer's product and this substantially lower wage, Fitzhugh explained, provided a measure of the exploited share of his work.

If this line of reasoning sounds familiar, it is due to a very real parallel between Fitzhugh's formulation of the capital–labor relationship and that of another famous contemporary. Fitzhugh had effectively worked out the Marxian theory of "surplus value" over a decade before the publication of Marx's own *Capital* (1867), and derived it from the same sweeping indictment of the free-labor capitalism.

The two thinkers would only diverge in their next steps, the prescriptive solution. Whereas Marx rejected chattel slavery and extrapolated a long historical march to an eventual socialist reordering through revolutionary upheaval, Fitzhugh saw a readily available alternative. "Slavery is a form, and the very best form, of socialism," he explained. Wage labor, he predicted, would be forever insufficient to meet the needs of the laborer due to deprivation of his products from his skill. Slavery, to Fitzhugh's convenience, could step in and fill the gap through the paternalistic provision of necessities for the enslaved, allegedly removing the "greed" of wage exploitation from the process.

Since slaves became the charge of the slave master and were placed under his care for food and shelter, Fitzhugh reasoned that "slaves consume more of the results of their own labor than laborers at the North." Plantation slavery, according to this contorted line of thinking, thereby mitigated the "exploitation" of wage labor capitalism and returned a greater portion of the posited surplus value. In the Marxian counterpart, a socialist state fulfills a similar function.

Fitzhugh's eccentric extrapolation from what are essentially Marxian doctrines has the effect of turning Marx's own untenable "solution" to capital ownership on its head. But the two thinkers unite in their grievances: a shared enmity toward market capitalism, and a desire to cast free market allocation of resources aside through coercive social reordering to achieve their respective ideal societies—mass enslavement or global communism.

These similarities between Fitzhugh and socialism, and indeed the aggressive anti-capitalist rhetoric of pro-slavery ideology, are seldom examined in the NHC literature. In its quest to politically tar modern capitalism with the horrors of slavery, these historians have adopted a practice of evidentiary negligence that conveniently excludes the explicit anti-capitalist ideological tenets of the very same slave system that they rebrand as a foundation of the modern capitalist economy.

Fitzhugh was not alone in adopting and adapting anti-capitalist ideology to the defense of slavery. Indeed, he heavily extrapolated it from Thomas Carlyle's own racist attacks upon the "dismal science" of economics on account of its close historical ties to abolitionism.[15] That these pro-slavery thinkers found a parallel rationale in socialism and deployed it to attack a common enemy of free markets, irrespective of their otherwise-divergent claims, is indicative of a shared illiberalism between the two. In practice, unfortunately, the immiserating historical records of each reveal that the only remaining distinction between their political outcomes consists of the choice between the slavery of the plantation and the slavery of the gulag.

....

15 Levy, David M. and Sandra J. Peart. 2001. "The Secret History of the Dismal Science. Part 1: Economics, Religion and Race in the 19th Century." *The Library of Economics and Liberty*, January 22.

How Capitalist-Abolitionists Fought Slavery

This article tells the little-known story of Lewis Tappan, a wealthy New York abolitionist who financed several of the most important publications and institutions in the American anti-slavery movement. Tappan's philanthropy caused an immense slaveholder backlash against his business interests. Rather than surrender to insolvency and ruin, he found a way to use free market institutions to circumvent a slaveholder boycott and slaveholder attempts to defraud his company.

* * *

Running afoul of slave-owning political interests almost destroyed brothers Lewis and Arthur Tappan, the wealthy owners of a prominent New York mercantile import business. On July 9, 1834, a pro-slavery mob gathered at New York City's Chatham Street Chapel with the intention of breaking up an abolitionist sermon.

Among their many grievances, the protesters were incensed at an incident some weeks earlier in which Arthur invited Rev. Samuel Cornish, an African American abolitionist and cofounder of the American Anti-Slavery Society, into his family pew for Sunday service. The gesture served as a powerful symbolic call for the racial integration of religious worship at the chapel. It also made the Tappan brothers— already well-known as a philanthropic force behind the abolitionist movement—the target of sensationalist conspiracy theorizing that spread to newspapers across the country and accused the devoutly Christian and pacifist brothers of fomenting a slave revolt.

Congregants caught wind of threats to forcibly disrupt their gathering and fled for their own safety. Still seeking a fight, the mob descended upon Lewis Tappan's nearby home, tossing its furniture into a fire on the street and successfully driving away an attempt by the New York police to quell the riot. For the next two days, breakaway mobs searched the city for the Tappan brothers, ransacking the homes both of white abolitionists and leaders of New York's free black community in the process. The same mobs attacked African-Americans on the streets at random and held crude racist political demonstrations in front of churches and businesses they deemed friendly to the abolitionist cause.

The Tappan brothers managed to escape relatively unscathed as the mayor stationed an armed militia to guard their storefront and drive away rioters. National news of the Chatham Incident, or "Tappan Riots" as they came to be called, carried other repercussions. It made the firm of Arthur Tappan & Co. into the target of a slave owner-instigated boycott that preyed upon public racism to drive away its customer base.

The mob targeting of the Tappans proved to be a watershed moment in the crusade to end slavery. William Lloyd Garrison's coverage of the riots demonstrated that slavery's defenders were willing to incite political violence in order to silence their critics. The episode also converted New York journalist William Leggett to the cause of abolition, which he then explicitly linked to a philosophy of laissez-faire capitalism and free trade.[16]

It also took a heavy toll on the Tappans' company. If the pro-slavery mob could not physically drive them from their New York business, it would destroy them nationally through a vilification campaign and economic targeting. Newspapers across the South demonized the brothers as the face of not only abolitionism but racial intermarriage, black political rights, and violent slave revolts. Groups of slave owners in New Orleans and Charleston even pledged a bounty on Arthur Tappan's head. A poster advertising a "$20,000 Reward for Tappan," for example, appears prominently in an 1835 depiction of slave owners ransacking a post office to intercept copies of William Lloyd Garrison's *The Liberator.*[17]

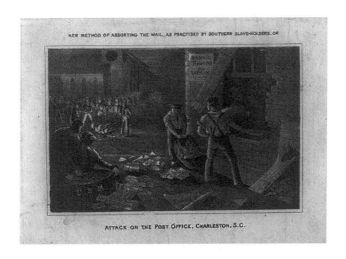

ATTACK ON THE POST OFFICE, CHARLESTON, S.C.

....

16 Magness, Phillip W. 2019. "William Leggett: Free Trade, Hard Money, and Abolitionism." *Online Library of Liberty*, July.

17 1853. *New Method of Assorting the Mail, as Practised by Southern Slave-Holders, Or Attack on the Post Office, Charleston, S.C.*

By 1837, the combined loss of business from the boycott and the descent of the American economy into a deep financial depression left the brothers owing more than $1 million to creditors. The decline represented a nearly complete reversal in fortunes for a firm previously known for its conservative bookkeeping and heavy reliance on cash transactions to limit its liabilities from customers who reneged on their payment obligations. Arthur Tappan & Co. finally closed shop.

Lewis Tappan, who often spoke of his business as a moral charge and who directed its proceeds in healthier times to a variety of abolitionist newspapers, was not yet ready to concede the fight to an orchestrated campaign of financial ruination. At his darkest moment, he came up with a brilliant plan that not only reversed his fortunes but also revolutionized the American financial industry.

Drawing on the experience of the boycott, Lewis recognized a systemic fault in the existing practices for business transactions carried out on credit. To fight back against a slave owner-incited boycott that undermined their cash purchases, the Tappans would reconstitute their business model around their existing network of connections in the abolitionist movement by offering credit transactions to trusted friends and associates. Establishing that trust, however, remained an obstacle, particularly if they ever hoped to expand this service beyond their own personal associations.

The complexities of the global import market and a growing customer base, spread across the nation's rapidly expanding geography, made the issuance of credit into an economic challenge. What was once a simple relationship between a shopkeeper and customers who were known to Lewis and who usually resided in his neighborhood now became a persistent information problem. With expanded markets, businesses could no longer afford to rely upon personal knowledge and reputation when vetting potential customers. A firm had to either insist upon payment up front or assume the risk that a customer would abscond with goods purchased on credit. The only available solutions were to pay for individual background checks on potential clients before extending them credit—an expensive and unwieldy undertaking for all but the largest of firms—or absorb the loss if a customer reneged on repayment.

Lewis Tappan devised an innovative solution to this problem by creating a service to independently track and validate the credit-worthiness of potential clients. In 1841 he founded the New York Mercantile Agency, the first modern credit-reporting firm in the United States. The new company offered a subscription-based service that collected and maintained a list of the credit-worthiness ratings of private businesses across New York City and, eventually, the country.

Reaching into his network of abolitionist connections and known clients from his old firm, Tappan was then able to assemble a network of credit investigators and attorneys who used local knowledge to assemble reports about outstanding debts, repayment rates, and defaults among the businesses in their cities and towns. A rating could then be provided to subscribers of the service, allowing them to reliably evaluate the risk of doing business with firms located thousands of miles away. The information problem at the root of previously complex credit arrangements could be mitigated through a market service that independently verified business reputations and conveyed their creditworthiness over long distances through simple consultation of a low-cost subscription paper.

Lewis Tappan's innovation revolutionized the American finance industry. The direct successor to his Mercantile Agency still exists today as Dun & Bradstreet, and his idea of an independent credit-reporting entity became the standard verification instrument of modern business lending and investment practices. The information it provided as an external and accessible measure of reputation, in turn, allowed for reliable and regular transactions to occur over long distances, thereby helping to ignite an unprecedented expansion of access to markets and goods across the nation.

The origins of Tappan's innovation remain a neglected feature in the history of American capitalism. A succinct account of the Mercantile Agency's history may be found in an article by historians Brian Grinder and Dan Cooper for the Museum of American Finance.[18] For a longer discussion, I recommend Roy A. Foulke's 1941 text *The Sinews of American Commerce,* which details its abolitionist origins.[19]

Their fortunes renewed, the Tappan brothers remained devoted benefactors of the abolitionist cause. After the Fugitive Slave Act of 1850 strengthened federal government efforts to recapture African-Americans in the North and return them to slavery, the brothers set up a network of lawyers to mount legal challenges to the renditions and, where possible, funneled money to support the Underground Railroad. Lewis also subsidized Lysander Spooner's book *The Unconstitutionality of Slavery* and financed the printing of his abolitionist pamphlets.[20]

Interest in the history of American capitalism is on the rise, although curiously this line of study is being advanced for anti-capitalistic

....

18 Grinder, Brian, and Dan Cooper. 2017. "Spies, Abolitionists and the Origins of Credit Rating Agencies." *Financial History,* (Winter,): 10-11 & 38.

19 Foulke, a vice president of Dun & Bradstreet, was also an early benefactor of the American Institute for Economic Research (AIER) and friend of E.C. Harwood. Foulke, Roy Anderson. 1896. *The Sinews of American Commerce.*

20 Letter and Envelope from L. Tappan to Lysander Spooner (1855, November 21st). New York Heritage Digital Collections.

ideological reasons as may be found in the *New York Times*' new 1619 Project on American slavery. Much of the associated academic literature, including sources used by the *Times*, relies on empirically shoddy and politicized lines of research that several leading economic historians have conclusively refuted.[21]

In eschewing factual analysis for political narratives, the scholars and journalists involved in the 1619 project appear to be far more interested in weaponizing the history of slavery with biased and even fabricated claims for the purpose of discrediting capitalism and free markets in the present day. They neglect the historical antagonism that existed between slave owners and free market capitalism, including a leading slavery defender who declared that capitalism was "at war with all kinds of slavery."[22]

It is therefore no small irony that one of the most important innovations in American financial history—the development of a reliable and replicable credit-reporting mechanism—owes its existence to a leading capitalist benefactor of the American anti-slavery movement. That innovation emerged as a tool for abolitionist business owners to escape violent harassment by racist mobs and coordinated economic targeting by plantation owners who sought to destroy the viability of their businesses. Lewis Tappan illustrated through his personal struggle and his economic entrepreneurship that American capitalism was, indeed, at war with slavery.

....

21 See chapter herein entitled "The Statistical Errors of the Reparations Agenda;" Olmstead, Alan L. and Paul W. Rhode. 2018. "Cotton, slavery, and the new history of capitalism." *Explorations in Economic History*, January; See chapter herein entitled "A Comment on the 'New' History of American Capitalism."

22 See chapter herein entitled "The Anti-Capitalist Ideology of Slavery."

The Statistical Errors of the Reparations Agenda

This article predates the 1619 Project by a few months, but touches directly on a faulty statistical claim that informs the broader New History of Capitalism (NHC) literature on which the Times relies. A widely repeated passage from a book by NHC historian Edward Baptist incorrectly asserts that slave-produced cotton accounted for almost half of the antebellum economy's gross domestic product (GDP). As I investigate and discuss, Baptist's claim is based on an elementary misunderstanding of how GDP is calculated that causes him to double- and triple-count several intermediate steps of cotton production. The actual share of antebellum GDP accounted for by cotton is closer to 5 percent.

* * *

Journalist and political commentator Ta-Nehisi Coates drew attention to the political cause of slavery reparations during a heavily publicized congressional hearing this week.[23] While commentators on both sides of the issue agree that his case was eloquently argued, one of its central claims rested on faulty economic data.

Specifically, Coates contends that the case for reparations comes from the economic measurement of the antebellum slave economy in the United States. He testified, "By 1836 more than $600 million, almost half of the economic activity in the United States, derived directly or indirectly from the cotton produced by the million-odd slaves."

This stunning statistical claim was widely repeated in commentary on the hearing. It is, however, unambiguously false.

Coates's numbers come from Cornell University historian Ed Baptist's 2014 book *The Half Has Never Been Told*.[24] In a key passage in the book, Baptist purports to add up the total value of economic activity that derived from cotton production, which at $77 million made up about 5 percent of the estimated gross domestic product (GDP) of the United States in 1836. Baptist then committed a fundamental accounting error. He proceeded to double and even triple count intermediate transactions involved in cotton production—things like land purchases for plantations, tools used for cotton production, transportation, insurance, and credit instruments used in each. Eventually that $77 million became $600 million in Baptist's accounting, or almost half of the entire antebellum economy of the United States.

There's a crucial problem with Baptist's approach. The calculation of GDP, the main formulation of national accounts and a representation

23 Paschal, Olivia and Madeleine Carlisle. 2019. "Read Ta-Nehisi Coates's Testimony on Reparations." *The Atlantic*, June 19.

24 Baptist, Edward E. 2014. *The Half Has Never Been Told: Slavery and the Making of American Capitalism*. New York: Basic Books.

of the dollar amount of economic activity in a country in a given year, only incorporates the value of final goods and services produced. The rationale for doing so comes from accounting, as the price of the final good already incorporates intermediate transactions that go into its production and distribution. Baptist's numbers are not only wrong—they reflect a basic unfamiliarity with the meaning and definition of GDP.

When *The Half Has Never Been Told* first appeared in print, economists immediately picked up on the error. Bradley Hansen of Mary Washington University kicked off the scrutiny by posting a thorough dissection of Baptist's errors on his personal blog.[25] Economic historians Alan Olmstead and Paul Rhode, of UC-Davis and the University of Michigan respectively, chimed in with a devastating critique of Baptist's empirics, observing that a continuation of his "faulty methodology by summing the 'roles' of cotton with a few other primary products" would yield an amount that "easily exceed[ed] 100 percent of GDP" in the antebellum United States—an economic impossibility.[26]

Stanley Engerman, perhaps the foremost living expert on the economics of slavery, weighed in next: [27]

....

25 Hanson, Bradley A. 2014. "The Back of Ed Baptist's Envelope." October 30. http://bradleyahansen.blogspot.com/2014/10/the-back-of-ed-baptists-envelope.html

26 Olmstead, Alan L. and Paul W. Rhode. 2018. "Cotton, slavery, and the new history of capitalism." *Explorations in Economic History*, January.

27 Fogel, Robert William and Stanley L. Engerman. 1995. *Time on the cross: The economics of American Negro slavery*. Vol. 1. WW Norton & Company; Engerman, Stanley L. 2017. "Review of 'The Business of Slavery and the Rise of American Capitalism, 1815-1860' by Calvin Schermerhorn and 'The Half Has Never Been Told: Slavery and the Making of American Capitalism' by Edward E. Baptist." *Journal of Economic Literature*, 55(2): 637-43.

Baptist's economic analysis, intended to demonstrate the essential role of the slave-grown cotton economy for Northern economic growth, is weakened by some variants of double- and triple-counting and some confusion of assets and income flows. To go from a value of the Southern cotton crop in 1836 of "about 5 percent of that entire gross domestic product," to "almost half of the economic activity of the United States in 1836" (pp 312-22) requires his calculation to resemble the great effects claimed by an NFL club when trying to convince city taxpayers that they should provide the money to build a new stadium because of all the stadium's presumed primary and secondary effects.

The main takeaways are that (1) the actual percentage of GDP derived from slavery is measured from final goods and services that involved slave-based production, and (2) Ed Baptist clearly did not understand what he was doing when he calculated his statistic. Cotton was by far the biggest item on the list of final goods and services, and, while its output varied year by year, it is probably reasonable to place slave-based goods in the mid to high single digits, not the 50 percent claim that Coates repeated.

Unfortunately, historians who work on the "New History of Cap-italism"—a school of historiography that emerged after the financial crisis of 2007–8 and that purports to study the relationship between slavery and capitalism—have proven remarkably ill-suited to grasping the fundamentals of GDP and other economic concepts.

Not to be outdone by Baptist's erroneous 50 percent estimate, Emory University historian Carol Anderson offered an even higher figure from the eve of the Civil War itself. According to Anderson, "80 percent of the nation's gross national product was tied to slavery" in 1860.

Following Coates's testimony using Baptist's erroneous numbers for 1836, several historians began circulating this estimate from Anderson's 2016 book *White Rage* as evidence of the growing influence of slavery on American capitalism in the late antebellum period.[28]

Like Baptist's book, it too derives from a fundamentally erroneous understanding of national accounts. Anderson's footnote points to the late historian David Brion Davis's foreword to a 2010 book on abolitionism. Davis makes a very different claim, however, in noting that the total value of slaves on the eve of the Civil War was equal to 80 percent of a *single year's* gross national product (GNP).[29] Anderson appears to have misread Davis's data point and transformed it into a broader claim about slavery's share of the entire economy.

While this figure is admittedly astounding and signifies the vast amount of wealth tied up in Southern slavery, Anderson mistakes it for the recurring *yearly* value of slave-produced economic output. She therefore commits the basic economic error of confusing stocks—by definition, a one-time measurement—and flows, which are measured over time. As we've already seen from Baptist's example though, the actual percentage of GDP (or GNP) tied up in slavery was actually a small fraction of that amount.

Basic statistical errors of this type are a pervasive feature of the "New History of Capitalism" genre of scholarship—even to the point that they are now entering into the discourse over policy discussions, as Coates's widely touted testimony at the reparations hearing illustrates.

....

28 Anderson, Carol. 2016. White Rage: The Unspoken Truth of Our Racial Divide. Bloomsbury.

29 Drescher, Seymour. (2010). *Econocide British Slavery in the Era of Abolition*. 2nd Ed., p. xiix.

In each case, the historians' demonstrably wrong GDP and GNP numbers make for a shocking claim that appears to situate slave production at the very core of all American economic activity before the Civil War. This claim appears to confirm many of the ideological expectations of the same historians, who also evince a pronounced hostility to market capitalism throughout their work. Linking historical capitalism to slavery is more of a political exercise for the present day than a scholarly inquiry into the past, and in fact the most virulent defenders of slavery in the mid-19th century actually presented their cause as an expressly anti-capitalist venture.[30]

There is a great moral gravity to discussions of slavery, not only as a historical problem but also an institution with persistent and adverse legacies that remain with us. It is therefore a timely and ever-present subject of scholarly inquiry and discussion. Regardless of where one stands on the reparations debate or other causes in the modern political scene, academics owe the public an honest, accurate, and scientific assessment of slavery's history, including its economic dimensions. That assessment is harmed when the discussion forgoes scientific rigor or even basic statistical practices to rally around a mistaken number in support of misleading and grossly inaccurate conclusions about the nature of the antebellum economy. Baptist, Coates, and the other public figures who have repeated this faulty statistic have an obligation to correct their error.

....

30 Fitzhugh, George. 1857. *Cannibals All! Or, Slaves Without Masters* (electronic ed.). Richmond: A. Morris, Publisher. https://docsouth.unc.edu/southlit/fitzhughcan/fitzcan.html at p. 79; Levy, David M. and Sandra J. Peart. 2001. "The Secret History of the Dismal Science. Part 1: Economics, Religion and Race in the 19th Century." *The Library of Economics and Liberty*, January 22.

Fact Checking the 1619 Project and Its Critics

I wrote this essay as an extended assessment of the debate between the historian critics of the 1619 Project and the Times's Jake Silverstein, following the simultaneous publication of each in the paper's letters section in December 2019. I evaluate each of the four contested claims and link to appropriate scholarly literature. Briefly, I find that (1) the historians have a stronger but not uncontested case on the role of slavery in the American Revolution, (2) the 1619 Project has a stronger argument on Abraham Lincoln, (3) the historians are correct to chastise the New History of Capitalism literature, and (4) the Times appears to have done an inadequate job at seeking scholarly guidance for the 1619 Project's sections on the American Revolution, slavery, and the Civil War, although it also did a much better job at externally vetting its claims on the 20th century and present day.

* * *

The *New York Times*'s 1619 Project entered a new phase of historical assessment when the paper published a scathing criticism by five well-known historians of the American Revolution and Civil War eras. The group included previous critics James McPherson, Gordon Wood, Victoria Bynum, and James Oakes, along with a new signature from Sean Wilentz. The newspaper's editor-in-chief Jake Silverstein then responded with a point-by-point rebuttal of the historians, defending the project.[31]

Each deserves to be taken seriously, as they form part of a larger debate on the merits of the 1619 Project as a work of history and its intended use in the K–12 classroom curriculum. While the project itself spans some four centuries, devoting substantial attention to racial discrimination against African-Americans in the present day, the historians' criticism focuses almost entirely on the two articles that are most directly pertinent to their own areas of expertise. The first is the lengthy introductory essay by Nikole Hannah-Jones, the *Times* journalist who edited the project. The second is a contentious essay on the relationship between slavery and American capitalism by Princeton University sociologist Matthew Desmond.

How should readers assess the competing claims of each group, seeing as they appear to be at bitter odds? That question is subject to a multitude of interpretive issues raised by the project's stated political aims, as well as the historians' own objectives as eminent figures— some might say gatekeepers—in the academic end of the profession.

But the debate may also be scored on its many disputed factual claims. To advance that discussion, I accordingly offer an assessment

....

31 We Respond to the Historians Who Critiqued The 1619 Project. *The New York Times*.

for each of the main points of contention as raised by the historians' letter and Silverstein's response.

1. WAS THE AMERICAN REVOLUTION FOUGHT IN DEFENSE OF SLAVERY?

One of the most hotly contested claims of the 1619 Project appears in its introductory essay by Nikole Hannah-Jones, who writes that "one of the primary reasons the colonists decided to declare their independence from Britain was because they wanted to protect the institution of slavery."

Hannah-Jones cites this claim to two historical events. The first is the 1772 British legal case of Somerset v. Stewart, which reasoned from English common law that a slave taken by his owner from the colonies to Great Britain could not be legally held against his will. England had never established slavery by positive law, therefore Somerset was free to go.

The second event she enlists is a late 1775 proclamation by Lord Dunmore, the colonial governor of Virginia, in which he offered freedom to slaves who would take up arms for the loyalist cause against the stirring rebellion.[32] The measure specified that it was "appertaining to Rebels" only, thereby exempting any slaves owned by loyalists.

Hannah-Jones argues that these two events revealed that British colonial rule presented an emerging threat to the continuation of slavery, thereby providing an impetus for slave-owning Americans to support independence. The American Revolution, she contends, was motivated in large part to "ensure slavery would continue." The five

....

32 1775. Transcription: Dunmore's Proclamation. November 7, 1775. *Library of Virginia.*

historians vigorously dispute this claimed causality, indicating that it exaggerates the influence of these events vis-à-vis better known objects of colonial ire, as stated in the *Declaration of Independence.*

There is a kernel of truth in Hannah-Jones's interpretation of these events. Somerset's case is traditionally seen as the starting point of Britain's own struggle for emancipation, and Dunmore's proclamation certainly provoked the ire of slave-owners in the southern colonies— although they were more likely to interpret it as an attempt to foment the threat of a slave revolt as a counter-revolutionary strategy than a sign that Britain itself would impose emancipation in the near future.

Curiously unmentioned in the dispute is a much clearer case of how the loyalist cause aligned itself with emancipation, albeit in a limited sense. As part of his evacuation of New York City in 1783, British commander Sir Guy Carleton secured the removal of over 3,000 slaves for resettlement in Nova Scotia. This action liberated more than ten times as many slaves as Dunmore's proclamation, the earlier measure having been offered as part of an increasingly desperate bid to retain power long after colonial opinion turned against him. Carleton's removal also became a source of recurring tensions for U.S.–British relations after the war's settlement. Alexander Hamilton, representing New York, even presented a resolution before the Con-federation Congress demanding the return of this human "property" to their former owners.[33]

That much noted, Hannah-Jones's argument must be assessed against the broader context of British emancipation. It is here that the five historians gain the stronger case. First, despite both its high

....

33 Magness, Phillip W. 2015. "Hamilton & Slavery, Part II." *Phillip W. Magness,* July 10. http://philmagness.com/?p=1330

symbolic importance and later use as a case precedent, the Somerset ruling was only narrowly applied as a matter of law. It did not portend impending emancipation across the empire, nor did its reach extend to either the American colonies or their West Indian neighbors where a much larger plantation economy still thrived.

It is also entirely unrealistic to speculate that Britain would have imposed emancipation in the American colonies had the war for independence gone the other way. We know this because Britain's own pathway to abolition in its remaining colonies entailed a half-century battle against intense parliamentary resistance after Somerset.

Simply securing a prohibition on the slave trade became a lifetime project of the abolitionist William Wilberforce, who proposed the notion in 1787, and of liberal Whig leader Charles James Fox, who brought it to a vote in 1791, only to see it go down in flames as merchant interests and West Indian planters organized to preserve the slave trade. Any student of the American Revolution will recognize the member of Parliament from Liverpool who successfully led the slave traders in opposition, for it was Banastre Tarleton, famed cavalry officer under General Cornwallis on the British side of the war.[34]

Tarleton's father and grandfather owned merchant firms in Liverpool, and directly profiteered from the slave trade. When Fox and Wilberforce's slave trade ban came to a vote he led the opposition in debate. The measure failed with 163 against and only 88 in favor.

After more than a decade of failed attempts Fox eventually persevered, steering a bill that allowed the slave trade ban through the House of Commons as one of his final acts before he died in 1806. It

....

34 Pocock, Nigel and Victoria Cook. 2011. "The Business of Enslavement." *British Broadcasting Corporation*, February 17.

would take another generation for Wilberforce and Thomas Clarkson, invested in a decades-long public campaign that highlighted the horrors of the institution and assisted by a large slave uprising in Jamaica, before a full Slavery Abolition Act would clear Parliament in 1833.

Nor was Tarleton the only loyalist from the revolutionary war with a stake in slavery as an institution. Lord Dunmore, whose 1775 proclamation forms the basis of the 1619 Project's argument, comes across as a desperate political opportunist rather than a principled actor once he is examined in light of his later career. From 1787 to 1796 he served as colonial governor of the Bahamas, where he embarked on a massive and controversial building project to fortify the city of Nassau against irrational fears of foreign invasion. Dunmore used more than 600 enslaved laborers to construct a network of fortifications, including a famous 66-step staircase that they hand carved from solid rock under the threat of whipping and torture.[35] Responding to a parliamentary inquiry on the condition of the colony's slaves in 1789, Dunmore absurdly depicted them as well cared for and content with their condition.[36]

Curiously enough, a British victory in the American Revolution would have almost certainly delayed the politics of this process even further. With the American colonies still intact, planters from Virginia, the Carolinas, and Georgia would have likely joined their West Indian counterparts to obstruct any measure that weakened slavery from advancing through Parliament. Subject to greater oversight from

....

35 The Islands of the Bahamas. 2020. "Queen's Staircase." *The Islands of the Bahamas.*

36 Documents of Parliament (UK). "Reports of the Lords of the Committee of Council appointed for the consideration of all matters relating to Trade and Foreign Plantations" 11 February 1788.

London, the northern colonies would have had fewer direct options to eliminate the institution on their own.

These state-initiated measures came about through both legislative action and legal proceeding, including a handful of "freedom cases" that successfully deployed reasoning similar to Somerset to strike against the presence of slavery in New England. The most notable example occurred in Massachusetts, where an escaped slave named Quock Walker successfully used the state's new post-independence Constitution of 1780 to challenge the legality of enforcing slavery within its borders.[37]

Although they had significantly smaller slave populations than the southern states, several other northern states used the occasion of independence to move against the institution. The newly constituted state governments of Pennsylvania (1780), New Hampshire (1783), Connecticut (1784), Rhode Island (1784), and New York (1799) adopted measures for gradual but certain emancipation, usually phased in over a specified period of time or taking effect as underage enslaved persons reached legal majority. Vermont abolished slavery under its constitution as an independent republic aligned with the revolutionaries in 1777, and officially joined the United States as a free state in 1791. Antislavery delegates to the Confederation Congress were similarly able to secure a prohibition against the institution's extension under the *Northwest Ordinance of 1787*, ensuring that the modern day states of Ohio, Michigan, Illinois, Wisconsin, and Indiana entered the Union

....

37 Historical document: "The Quock Walker case: "Instructions to the Jury"". 1783. Public Broadcasting Service.

as free states.[38]

While these examples do not negate the pernicious effects of slavery upon the political trajectory of the former southern colonies, they do reveal clear instances where the cause of emancipation was aided—rather than impeded—by the American Revolution. Britain's own plodding course to emancipation similarly negates an underlying premise of Hannah-Jones' depiction of the Crown as an existential threat to American slavery itself in 1776. Indeed, the reluctance of the slaveholding West Indian colonies to join those on the continent in rebellion despite repeated overtures from the Americans reveals the opposite. The planters of Jamaica, Barbados and other Caribbean islands considered their institutions secure under the Crown—and they would remain so for another half-century.

The Verdict: The historians have a clear upper hand in disputing the portrayal of the American Revolution as an attempt to protect slavery from British-instigated abolitionism. Britain itself remained several decades away from abolition at the time of the revolution. Hannah-Jones's argument nonetheless contains kernels of truth that complicate the historians' assessment, without overturning it. Included among these are instances where Britain was involved in the emancipation of slaves during the course of the war. These events must also be balanced against the fact that American independence created new opportunities for the northern states to abolish slavery within

....

38 "The Northwest Ordinance." 1787. *National Archives,* Records of the Continental and Confederation Congresses and the Constitutional Convention, 1774-1789: Miscellaneous Papers (Microfilm Publication M332, roll 9, Record Group 360). Passed July 13, 1787.

their borders. In the end, slavery's relationship with the American Revolution was fraught with complexities that cut across the political dimensions of both sides.

2. WAS ABRAHAM LINCOLN A RACIAL COLONIZATIONIST OR EXAGGERATED EGALITARIAN?

In her lead essay, Nikole Hannah-Jones pointed to several complexities in the political beliefs of Abraham Lincoln to argue that his reputation as a racial egalitarian has been exaggerated. She points specifically to Lincoln's longstanding support for the colonization of freed slaves abroad as a corollary feature of ending slavery, including a notorious August 1862 meeting at the White House in which the President pressed this scheme upon a delegation of free African-Americans.

Elsewhere she points to grating remarks by Lincoln that questioned the possibility of attaining racial equality in the United States, and to his tepid reactions to the proposition of black citizenship at the end of the Civil War. Hannah-Jones's final assessment is not unduly harsh, but it does dampen some of the "Great Emancipator" mythology of popular perception while also questioning the extent to which Lincoln can be viewed as a philosophical egalitarian, as distinct from an anti-slavery man.

The historians' letter contests this depiction, responding that Lincoln evolved in an egalitarian direction and pointing to his embrace of an anti-slavery constitutionalism that was also shared by Frederick Douglass. Hannah-Jones, they contend, has essentially cherry picked quotations and other examples of Lincoln's shortcomings on racial matters and presented them out of context from his life and broader philosophical principles.

Although the historians' letter to the *Times* only briefly discusses the particular details of Hannah-Jones's essay, several of the signers have individually elaborated on these claims. McPherson, Oakes, and Wilentz have all advanced various interpretations that imbue Lincoln with more radical sentiments—including on racial equality—than his words and actions evince at the surface.[39]

These arguments usually depict an element of political shrewdness at play in which Lincoln is forced to obscure his true intentions from a racist electorate until emancipation was secured or the Civil War was won. When Hannah-Jones points to policies such as colonization, or to problematic speeches by Lincoln that suggest a less-than-egalitarian view of African-Americans, the historians respond that these charges miss a deeper political context. And in their telling, that context largely serves an exonerative purpose.

The historians' treatment of colonization is probably the foremost example of how they deploy this argument around Lincoln. McPherson was one of the main originators of what has become known as the "lullaby thesis".[40] According to this thesis, Lincoln only advanced racially charged policies such as colonization to lull a reluctant populace into accepting the "strong pill" of emancipation. Once emancipation was achieved, McPherson and the other lullaby theorists maintain, Lincoln promptly retreated from these racially fraught auxiliary positions—a claim supposedly evidenced by Lincoln's omission of colonizationist language from the final version of the *Emancipation*

....

39 McPherson, James M. 1982. *Ordeal by Fire: The Civil War and reconstruction.*

40 See McPherson, James M. (1982); Magness, Phillip W. and Sebastian N. Page. 2011. *Colonization After Emancipation: Lincoln and the Movement for Black Resettlement.*

Proclamation of January 1, 1863. Colonization is therefore reduced to a political stratagem, insincerely advanced to clear the way for emancipation.

Wilentz echoes McPherson on this claim, and at times presses it even further. In 2009 he published a vicious and dismissive attack on Henry Louis Gates, Jr., after the eminent African-American scholar called upon historians to update their consideration of Lincoln's colonization policies and consider the possibility that they sincerely reflected his beliefs.[41]

Gates's interpretation was far from radical or disparaging of Lincoln.[42] He correctly noted that the evidentiary record on Lincoln's colonization programs had substantially expanded since the time that McPherson and others posited the lullaby thesis in the second half of the 20th century. Wilentz's counter-argument offered little to counter the new evidence, relying instead on invocations of authority from leading scholars including himself.[43]

When viewed in light of these and other recent archival discoveries, the lullaby thesis and similar variants as espoused by the signers of the letter may be conclusively rejected.

Lincoln's sincere belief in colonization may be documented from the earliest days of his political career as a Henry Clay Whig in Illinois to

....

41 Wilentz, Sean. 2009. "Who Lincoln Was." *The New Republic*, July 15.

42 Gates, Henry Louis Jr. 2009. *Lincoln on Race and Slavery.* Princeton: Princeton University Press.

43 I was one of the principal co-discoverers of the new materials, including several large caches of diplomatic records from Lincoln's efforts to secure sites for freedmen's colonies in the West Indies that are now housed in Great Britain, Belize, the Netherlands, and Jamaica. 2011. "Lincoln urged free blacks to resettle abroad." *CBS News*, March 4.

a succession of failed attempts to launch colonization projects during his presidency.[44] Furthermore, the claim that Lincoln abandoned colonization after the *Emancipation Proclamation* in January 1863 is directly belied by another year of sustained diplomatic negotiations with the governments of Great Britain and the Netherlands as Lincoln sought to secure suitable locales in their Caribbean colonies.[45]

Lincoln's proactive support for colonization kept it alive until at least 1864 when a series of political setbacks induced Congress to strip away the program's funding against the President's wishes. A fair amount of evidence suggests Lincoln intended to revive the project in his second term, and new discoveries pertaining to long-missing colonization records from Lincoln's presidency continue to be made.[46]

I won't belabor the point further, save to note that the evidence of

....

44 Magness, Phillip W. 2015. "The American System and the Political Economy of Black." *Journal of the History of Economic Thought, 37*(2): 187-202. doi:10.1017/S1053837215000206; Magness, Phillip W. 2012. "Wither Liberia? Civil War Emancipation and Freedmen Resettlement in West Africa." *The Civil War Monitor*, November 11; Magness, Phillip W. 2013. "The Île à Vache: From Hope to Disaster." *The New York Times,* Opinion Pages, April 12; Page, Sebastian N. 2011. "Lincoln and Chiriquí Colonization Revisited." *American Nineteenth Century History*, 12(3): 289-325.

45 Page, Sebastian. 2012. "Lincoln, Colonization and the Sound of Silence." *The New York Times*, Opinion Pages, December 4; Magness and Page (2011); Douma, Michal J. 2019. *The Colonization of Freed African Americans in Suriname: Archival Sources Relating to the U.S. Dutch Negotiations, 1860-1866.* Leiden University Press; Douma, Michal J. 2015. "The Lincoln Administration's Negotiations to Colonize African Americans in Dutch Suriname." *Civil War History*, 61(2): 111-137; Magness, Phillip W. 2012. "The British Honduras Colony: Black Emigrationist Support for Colonization in the Lincoln Presidency." *Slavery & Abolition*, 34(1): 39-69.

46 Magness, Phillip W. 2015. "Lincoln and the case for Ben Butler's Colonization Story." *Phillip W. Magness.* April 16. http://philmagness.com/?p=1213; Magness, Phillip W. 2011. "James Mitchell and the Mystery of the Emigration Office Papers." *Journal of the Abraham Lincoln Association*, 32(2): 50-62.

Lincoln's sincere support for colonization is overwhelming.[47]

This finding carries with it the substantial caveat that Lincoln did not pursue this course out of personal racial animosity. Quite the contrary, his public and private statements consistently link the policy to his personal fears that former slave-owners would continue to oppress African-Americans after the Civil War. The colonization component of his solution was a racially retrograde and paternalistic reflection of its time, but it also revealed Lincoln's awareness of the challenges that lay ahead in his second term. Given that Lincoln's presidency and life were cut short, we will never know what that term would have brought. And while there are subtle clues of Lincoln's migration toward greater racial inclusivity in other areas—for example, the extension of suffrage to black soldiers—the record on colonization is in clear tension with the arguments advanced by the 1619 Project's critics.

The Verdict: Nikole Hannah-Jones has the clear upper hand here. Her call to evaluate Lincoln's record through problematic racial policies such as colonization reflects greater historical nuance and closer attention to the evidentiary record, including new developments in Lincoln scholarship. The historians' counter-arguments reflect a combination of outdated evidence and the construction of apocryphal exonerative narratives such as the lullaby thesis around colonization.

....

47 See Magness, Phillip W. 2016. "Abraham Lincoln and Colonization." *Essential Civil War Curriculum*, February, pp. 1-17.

3. DID SLAVERY DRIVE AMERICA'S ECONOMIC GROWTH AND THE EMERGENCE OF AMERICAN CAPITALISM?

Matthew Desmond's 1619 Project contribution has been at the center of the firestorm since the day it was published.[48] The main thrust of this article holds that slavery was the primary driver of American economic growth in the 19th century, and that it infused its brutality into American capitalism today. The resulting thesis is overtly ideological and overtly anti-capitalist, seeking to enlist slavery as an explanatory mechanism for a long list of grievances he has against the Republican Party's positions on healthcare, taxation, and labor regulation in the present day.

The five historians directly challenged the historical accuracy of Desmond's thesis. By presenting "supposed direct connections between slavery and modern corporate practices," they note, the 1619 Project's editors "have so far failed to establish any empirical veracity or reliability" of these claims "and have been seriously challenged by other historians." The historians' letter further chastises the *Times* for extending its "imprimatur and credibility" to these claims.

Each of these criticisms rings true.

Desmond's thesis relies exclusively on scholarship from a hotly contested school of thought known as the New History of Capitalism (NHC). Although NHC scholars often present their work as cutting-edge explorations into the relationship between capitalism and slavery, they have not fared well under scrutiny from outside their

....

48 Desmond, Matthew. 2019. "American Capitalism is Brutal. You Can Trace That to the Plantation." *The New York Times*, August 14.

own ranks.[49]

Other scholars, including several leading economic historians, have reached similar conclusions, finding very little merit in this body of work. As discussed in previous sections of this book, the NHC camp frequently struggles with basic economic concepts and statistics, has a clear track record of misrepresenting historical evidence to bolster its arguments, and has adopted a bizarre and insular practice of refusing to answer substantive scholarly criticisms from non-NHC scholars—including from opposite ends of the political spectrum.[50]

While most criticisms of Desmond's thesis focus upon these broader problems in the NHC literature, the *Times* has done practically nothing to address the issues involved. Hannah-Jones herself admitted to being unaware of the controversy surrounding the NHC material until I pointed it out to her shortly after the 1619 Project appeared in print.[51] From that time until the present the 1619 Project has almost intentionally disengaged from the problems with Desmond's essay—and so it remains in Silverstein's response.

Although the *Times* editor attempted to answer most of the other

....

49 Magness, Phillip W. 2019. "How the 1619 Project Rehabilitates the 'King Cotton' Thesis." *National Review*, August 26; Clegg, John J. 2015. "Capitalism and Slavery." *Critical Historical Studies*, 2(2): 281-304; McCloskey, Deirdre N. 2018. "Slavery Did Not Make America Rich." *Reason*, August/September

50 Magness, Phillip W. 2019. "The Statistical Errors of the Reparations Agenda." *American Institute for Economic Research*, June 23; Olmstead, Alan L. and Paul W. Rhode. 2018. "Cotton, slavery, and the new history of capitalism." *Explorations in Economic History*, January; See chapter herein entitled "The New History of Capitalism Has a 'Whiteness' Problem;" Clegg, John J. 2019. "How Slavery Shaped American Capitalism." *Jacobin*, August 28.

51 Hannah-Jones, Nikole. 2019. "Economists dispute a few of Baptist's calculations but not the book itself nor its thesis." Twitter, August 18, 2019. https://twitter.com/nhannahjones/status/1163030801778401281

specific criticisms from the historians, he was conspicuously silent on the subject of Desmond's thesis. Hannah-Jones has similarly shown little interest in revisiting this piece or responding to specific criticisms of the NHC literature. Meanwhile, the *Times* continues to extend this defective body of academic work its imprimatur and credibility, exactly as the historians' letter charges.

The Verdict: This one goes conclusively to the five historians. Echoing other critics, the historians point to serious and substantive defects with Matthew Desmond's thesis about the economics of slavery, and with the project's overreliance on the contested New History of Capitalism literature. By contrast, the *Times* has completely failed to offer a convincing response to this criticism—or really any response at all.

4. DID THE 1619 PROJECT SEEK ADEQUATE SCHOLARLY GUIDANCE IN PREPARING ITS WORK?

Moving beyond the content of the project itself, the historians' letter raises a broader criticism of the scholarly vetting behind the 1619 Project. They charge that the *Times* used an "opaque" fact-checking process, marred by "selective transparency" about the names and qualifications of scholars involved. They further suggest that Hannah-Jones and other *Times* editors did not solicit sufficient input from experts on the subjects they covered—a point that several of the signers reiterated in their individual interviews.

Silverstein takes issue with this criticism, noting that they "consulted with numerous scholars of African-American history and related fields" and subjected the resulting articles to rigorous fact-checking. He also specifically identifies five scholars involved in these consultations who each contributed a piece to the 1619 Project. They are Mehrsa Baradaran, Matthew Desmond, Kevin Kruse, Tiya Miles, and Khalil G. Muhammed.

Each of these scholars brings relevant areas of expertise to aspects of the larger project. The listed names, however, are noticeably light when it comes to historians of the subject areas that the critics describe as deficient, namely the period from the American Revolution to the Civil War or roughly 1775 to 1865.

Of the five named academic consultants, only Miles possesses a clear scholarly expertise in this period of history. Her contributions to the project—three short vignettes about slavery, business, and migration—are not disputed by the five historian critics, and do not appear to have elicited any significant criticism.[52] Rather, they have been well-received as abbreviated distillations of her scholarly work for a popular audience.

The true oddity of the group remains Matthew Desmond, a sociologist who specializes in present day race-relations. Although Desmond was given the task of writing the 1619 Project's main article on the economics of slavery, he does not appear to have any scholarly expertise in either economics or the history of slavery. None of his scholarly publications are on subjects related to the period between 1775 and 1865.[53] Indeed most of his work focuses on the 20th century or later. As a result, Desmond approaches his 1619 Project essay entirely as

....

52 Miles, Tiya. 2019. "Chained Migration: How Slavery Made Its Way West.", "How Slavery Made Wall Street" and "The Enslaved Pecan Pioneer." In The 1619 Project, *The New York Times Magazine*, August 14, 2019.

53 Desmond, Matthew. 2020. "Matthew Desmond Publications." https://scholar.princeton.edu/matthewdesmond/publications-0

a second-hand disseminator of the aforementioned claims from the problematic New History of Capitalism literature.

The other three named consultants—Kruse, Baradaran, and Muhammad—all specialize in more recent areas of history or social science, so none of them could plausibly claim an expertise in the period that the five historians focus their criticisms upon.

Barring the revelation of additional names, it appears that the 1619 Project neglected to adequately vet its material covering slavery during the period between the American Revolution and the Civil War. Its editors also appear to have assigned the primary article on this period to a writer who may possess expertise in other areas of social science involving race, but who is not qualified for the specific task of assessing slavery's economic dimensions.

Although Silverstein attempted to defuse this angle of the historians' criticism, he ended up only affirming its validity. Since the period in question encompasses several of the most important events in the history of slavery, this oversight harms the project's credibility in the areas where the five historians are highly regarded experts.

The Verdict: The historians have a valid complaint about deficiencies of scholarly guidance for the 1619 Project's treatment of the period between the American Revolution and the Civil War. This comparative lack of scholarly input for the years between 1775 and 1865 stands in contrast with the *Times'* heavy use of scholars who specialize in more recent dimensions of race in the United States. It is worth noting that the 1619 Project has received far less pushback on its materials about the 20th century and present day—areas that are more clearly within the scholarly competencies of the named consultants

The Case for Retracting Matthew Desmond's 1619 Project Essay

In a series of exchanges with 1619 Project editor Nikole Hannah-Jones, I first raised the possibility of the Times issuing a correction to the many factual errors in Matthew Desmond's essay on capitalism and slavery. As I noted at the time, substantively addressing the problems with this piece alone would resolve several of the most severe criticisms of the project as a whole. It would also be consistent with the Times's reputation for vigorous fact-checking.

The faults with Desmond's essay extended beyond the interpretive disputes of the other contributions, and included both factual errors and misrepresentations of claims that appeared in scholarly works of history and economic history. After multiple attempts to pursue these corrections through the Times yielded little response and continued dismissiveness about the problems by Hannah-Jones, I summarized the main faults in an essay calling for the retraction of Desmond's piece.

* * *

Since the outset of the 1619 Project controversy detailed throughout this book, I have consistently argued that the overwhelming majority of the project's problems derive from a single featured essay: Matthew Desmond's piece on capitalism and slavery.[54]

Desmond's essay advances an explicit anti-capitalist political message that's rooted in a fundamental misreading of economic history. Although he repurposes the concept with an anti-slavery message, Desmond essentially attempts to rehabilitate "King Cotton" ideology, a long-discredited piece of pro-slavery propaganda from the Confederate era. He also ignores the aforementioned intellectual history of capitalism, including the strong historical association between laissez-faire theorists and abolitionism.

I'd like to take a look at another dimension of the problems in Desmond's essay: its errors of historical fact and its misuse of historical sources.

In doing so, it is important to recognize that there are still faults with other contributions to the 1619 Project. Its lead essay still exaggerates British anti-slavery elements during the American Revolution, repurposing independence as a pro-slavery movement.[55] But these faults are not irremediable. They could be addressed by relaxing the claim or injecting greater nuance into the discussion, should the *Times* exhibit an inclination to place historical accuracy above politics.

....

54 Desmond, Matthew. 2019. "American Capitalism is Brutal. You Can Trace That to the Plantation." *The New York Times*, August 14.

55 Hannah-Jones, Nikole. 2019. "America Wasn't a Democracy Until Black Americans Made It One." *New York Times*, August 14, 2019; Young, Cathy. 2020. "The Fight Over the 1619 Project." *The Bulwark*, February 9, 2020.

Desmond's argument, however, is riddled with factual error and dubious scholarly interpretations that warrant severely discounting the piece as a whole.

Let's consider those problems.

A Faulty Genealogy

Desmond begins his argument by asserting a direct lineal descent from the violent and coercive operations of the plantation system to the business practices of the modern economy. As he contends, "recently, historians have pointed persuasively to the gnatty fields of Georgia and Alabama, to the cotton houses and slave auction blocks, as the birthplace of America's low-road approach to capitalism." The historians he refers to here are almost exclusively drawn from the highly contested "New History of Capitalism" (NHC) school, and many of its leading contributors are featured in his essay.

Desmond's reliance on such a narrow historiographical echo chamber is itself problematic, given how many scholars outside of the NHC reject its claims and given the documentation of errors affecting its core claims. We may nonetheless follow his claimed genealogical progression from the plantation to the modern economy. The effect of this alleged infusion, Desmond therefore contends, is to instill modern capitalism with a foundational "brutality" that can only be rectified by adopting a litany of economic policy interventions that bear striking resemblance to the progressive wing of the Democratic Party today.

The stated genealogy is presented as a matter of fact. Desmond invokes the imagery of a modern corporation where "everything is tracked, recorded and analyzed, via vertical reporting systems, double-entry record-keeping and precise quantification," then asserts that "many of these techniques that we now take for granted were developed by and for large plantations."

"When an accountant depreciates an asset to save on taxes or when a mid-level manager spends an afternoon filling in rows and columns on an Excel spreadsheet," he continues, "they are repeating business procedures whose roots twist back to slave-labor camps." By direct implication, modern capitalism carries that same moral stain with it.

There are immediate problems with Desmond's historical narrative. The history of double-entry bookkeeping and business measurement predates plantation slavery by several centuries, with origins that are directly traceable to the banking families of late medieval Italy.[56] Desmond seems not to understand the accounting function of depreciation, which arose mainly in the railroad industry as a mechanism for distributing the distortive effects of large replacement purchases on machinery that underwent constant wear and tear.[57]

Nor are the tools of measurement and finance distinctly capitalistic, as their attempted adaptation to the centralized planning of the Soviet Union and other 20th century communist states attests. Most attempts to operationalize socialist economic planning depend by necessity on the complex quantification of resource allocation, or attempts at input-output modeling of inter-industry relationships, usually adopted as an alternative to the obviated role of the price mechanism in decentralized

....

56 Gleeson-White, Jane. 2012. *Double Entry: How the Merchants of Venice Created Modern Finance.* W.W. Norton.

57 Brazell, David W., Lowell Dworin and Michal Walsh. 1989. "A History of Federal Tax Depreciation Policy." *U.S. Treasury Department,* Office of Tax Analysis Paper 64.

allocation.[58]

But even more problematically, Desmond's claim does not match his own stated source, Caitlin Rosenthal's 2018 book *Accounting for Slavery*.[59] While Rosenthal does investigate the historical use of accounting practices on the plantation with informative insights into how slave owners made their institution profitable, she attaches a substantial caveat at the outset of her book:

> This is not an origins story. I did not find a simple path where slaveholders' paper spreadsheets evolved into Microsoft Excel.

The plain language of this caveat expressly disavows the genealogical interpretation that Desmond assigns to her work, even using the very same example of Microsoft Excel to convey her rejection. In short, the 1619 Project inverts its source's claimed purpose.

When I recently pointed this contradiction out to the *Times*, the newspaper's editors indicated that they were standing by Desmond's claim nonetheless and suggested that doing so now meets with Rosenthal's own post hoc concurrence. Given that her publisher is also now touting Desmond's passage as an endorsement of this book, one is left to wonder why this caveat was included if it is going to be abandoned with such nonchalance.

....

58 Kantorovich, L. V. 1939. *Mathematical Methods of Organizing and Planning Production*; Nobel Media AB. 2020. "The Sveriges Riksbank Prize in Economic Sciences in Memory of Alfred Nobel 1973." *The Nobel Prize*; Mises, Ludwig von. 1981. *Socialism: An Economic and Sociological Analysis*. Indianapolis: Liberty Fund. Translated by J. Kahane.

59 Rosenthal, Caitlin. 2018. *Accounting for Slavery*. Cambridge: Harvard University Press. See p. xii.

The alteration carries substantial implications for Rosenthal's thesis. As presented in its original form, *Accounting for Slavery* documents the unsurprising but historically interesting fact that slave owners managed their plantations by adapting then-modern accounting and financial practices found elsewhere in the business community to their own horrid institution.

When repurposed as a genealogy, however, this thesis falls apart for want of evidence. Rosenthal's work does not show that the specific accounting practices of the plantations were transmitted to modern Wall Street, or that later businessmen learned their trades specifically from slavery's financial innovations, as opposed to common financial and accounting practices that long predate the American plantation system. If accepted, Desmond's rendering of *Accounting for Slavery* would damage its own scholarly contribution as a work of history by stretching its evidence far beyond what the book's contents and documentation either claim or support. Yet that's the reading the *Times* appears to be sticking with.

Even in this simple presentation, Desmond's spin on Rosenthal's work exhibits the telltale characteristics of the genetic fallacy, wherein an unsavory origin is said to be a discrediting of a position in the present. But Desmond's origin story is also wrong.

Illustrative of this fallacy, he quotes NHC historians Sven Beckert and Seth Rockman to assert that "American slavery is necessarily imprinted on the DNA of American capitalism." Beckert and Rockman's genetic claim would have come as a great surprise, if not a source of outrage, to the slaveholders of the late antebellum period. As mentioned earlier, leading pro-slavery theorist George Fitzhugh wrote in 1854 that the tenets of free market capitalism were "at war with all kinds of slavery, for they in fact assert that individuals and peoples prosper most when governed least."[60] The depiction of slavery as capitalistic also chafes with the most developed ideological justifications that Southern radicals made for their economic system—a system built upon a coerced hierarchy of laborers forced to do menial tasks under the paternalistic direction of quasi-feudal plantation owners.[61]

This leaves Desmond's historical account fraught through with factual and interpretive errors. His attempt to tie slavery to modern accounting misses the latter's known and separate origins, misrepresents accounting and measurement as uniquely capitalistic, and directly inverts the disavowal of an origin story in its own cited source.[62] It's safe to say that his thesis is off to a poor start.

A Misrepresented Statistical Claim

Taking his own false genealogy of modern accounting as a given, Desmond next turns to its claimed economic implications for the plantation system. To illustrate the effect, he points to a stunning statistic:

> During the 60 years leading up to the Civil War, the daily amount of cotton picked per enslaved worker increased 2.3 percent a year. That means that in 1862, the average enslaved fieldworker picked not 25 percent or 50 percent as much but 400 percent as much cotton than his or her counterpart did in 1801.

....

60 Fitzhugh, George. 1854. *Sociology for the South Or The Failure of Free Society* (electronic ed.). Richmond: A. Morris, Publisher.

61 Speech of James Henry Hammond. 1858. "On the Admission of Kansas, Under the Lecompton Constitution" (also known as the "Cotton is King"). *American Antiquarian Society.*

62 Eicholz, Hans. 2019. "Slavery Gave Us Double-Entry Bookkeeping?" *Law and Liberty*, October 2.

The implication is clear. Desmond seeks to convey that "capitalist" business practices allowed plantation masters to forcibly extract the maximum amount of productivity from their enslaved workforce to such a degree that it causally drove the rapid expansion of the American cotton industry in the early 19th century. Cotton output, he contends, arose directly from a symbiotic convergence of capitalism and the whip.

The underlying statistic is nominally accurate insofar as American cotton production grew almost fourfold between 1800 and the Civil War. But Desmond has also repeated a severe misrepresentation of this statistic's source.

The 400 percent increase estimate comes from a 2008 article by economists Alan Olmstead and Paul Rhode, and reflects their calculation of yearly cotton picking rates from almost 150 sets of plantation records.[63] Yet Olmstead and Rhode do not attribute this production increase to a devil's bargain between double-entry bookkeeping and systematized beatings of the slaves. Instead, they present clear evidence of a very different explanation. American planters improved their crop through biological innovation, such as creating hybrid seed strains that yielded more cotton, were easier to pick, and were more resistant to disease. As Olmstead and Rhode conclude:

> Technological changes revolutionized southern cotton production in the 60 years preceding the Civil War. The amount of cotton a typical slave picked per day increased about 2.3 percent per year due, primarily, to the introduction and perfection of superior cotton varieties.

....

63 Olmstead, Alan L. and Paul W. Rhode. 2008. "Biological Innovation and Productivity Growth in the Antebellum Cotton Economy." *Working Paper,* June.

Although the two economists support this technological explanation with extensive statistical evidence, Desmond and the NHC scholars he relies on ignore it and append their own alternative spin to Olmstead and Rhode's data. Instead of seed improvements, they contend that the 400 percent increase arose from a systematized and quantified process of whipping meant to extract greater labor from the slaves.

Desmond gets this alternative interpretation directly from NHC historian Ed Baptist. According to Baptist, the Olmstead and Rhode statistics attest to "an economy whose bottom gear was torture." By tracking individual slave production, he contends, slave drivers were essentially able to calibrate their torture to maximize and increase cotton picking rates over time. As Desmond describes it, "The violence [of slavery] was neither arbitrary nor gratuitous. It was rational, capitalistic, all part of the plantation's design."

The "calibrated torture" thesis is a central claim of Baptist's 2015 book *The Half Has Never Been Told,* itself one of the foundational texts of the NHC genre.[64] Turning to Baptist's book, we find clearly that he too enlisted Olmstead and Rhode's 2008 paper for his evidence of the fourfold increase in cotton output before the Civil War, even reprinting one of their main graphs on page 127 of his book and another of their tables on page 129.

Baptist's book is an unscholarly mess of misinterpreted data, misrepresented sources, and empirical incompetence. In proclaiming the novelty of its own "never told" story, he also constructs a bizarre strawman of the scholarly literature on the economics of slavery before

....

64 Hansen, Bradley A. 2018. "Stop Telling Kanye to Read Ed Baptist." *Bradley A. Hansen's Blog,* May 3; Hansen, Bradley A. 2019. "A Description of the Problems with Edward Baptist's "The Half Has Never Been Told" for Non-Economists." *Bradley A. Hansen's Blog,* September 2.

his own work. As Baptist writes on page 129 of his book, the claim that slavery was less efficient than free labor is "a point of dogma that most historians and economists have accepted."

In reality, most economic historians have associated economic efficiency as well as profitability with slavery since a landmark article by Alfred Conrad and John R. Meyer argued this position in 1958.[65] The relationship between slavery, efficiency, and profitability is the subject of a vast subsequent literature that Baptist almost entirely ignores.[66] As we can already see, his book is essentially arguing against a phantasm of his own imagination.

The problems similarly extend to Baptist's treatment of the Olmstead and Rhode data. Although Baptist uses the economists' statistics, he conveniently omits their evidence that cotton production growth arose from biological innovation in seed strains. Instead he supplants it with his own explanation, the "calibrated torture" thesis that Desmond then repeats. In the NHC telling, the 400 percent growth in cotton output arose from "ratcheting" production rates upward through tracked and mathematized beatings of the slaves who picked the crop.

Baptist's sleight of hand was not lost upon the economists. In 2018 Olmstead and Rhode published a withering rebuttal of Baptist's book,

....

65 Conrad, Afred H and John R Meyer. 1958. "The Economics of Slavery in the Ante Bellum South." *Journal of Political Economy*, 66(2): 95-130.

66 Hummel, Jeffrey. 2012. "Deadweight Loss and the American Civil War: The Political Economy of Slaver, Secession, and Emancipation." (October 1); Belotta, Tony. "Robert Fogel and Stanley Engerman's Time on the Cross: The Economics of American Negro Slavery 1974 with Phillip W. Magness." *The Age of Jackson Podcast,* podcast number 090 (January 2017); Engerman, Stanley L. 2017. "Review of 'The Business of Slavery and the Rise of American Capitalism, 1815-1860' by Calvin Schermerhorn and 'The Half Has Never Been Told: Slavery and the Making of American Capitalism' by Edward E. Baptist." *Journal of Economic Literature*, 55(2): 637-43.

using additional records from plantations to empirically debunk his "calibrated torture" argument.[67] Rather than corresponding to mathematized whipping—a claim that Baptist also makes by altering and distorting the text of historical slave narratives to make them fit his thesis—actual cotton picking rates from the Olmstead and Rhode data clearly follow a seasonal pattern corresponding to the annual crop cycle. As the economists write:

> Recall that Baptist has embraced our data showing a roughly four fold increase in average cotton picking rates over the antebellum years. These data only reported plantation yearly averages. If we turn up the power of our microscope and look at the daily data for individual slaves that we used to construct the plantation averages, a whole new world appears that allows us to investigate empirically the effect of current picking on future picking. There is no evidence of ratcheting. Over the course of a year picking rates formed an inverted "U" going up to a peak period and then falling significantly.

In short, Baptist's thesis not only misrepresents the evidence from Olmstead and Rhode, his own cited data source—it also misunderstands the numbers behind that source.

Baptist, much to the discredit of his professionalism, has subsequently adopted a strategy of refusing to engage with Olmstead and Rhode's rebuttal. Instead he brushes it aside and persists as if his own thesis is uninterrupted and unaltered in the face of clear contradictory evidence.

....

67 Olmstead, Alan L. and Paul W. Rhode. 2018. "Cotton, slavery, and the new history of capitalism." *Explorations in Economic History*, January.

Although the 1619 Project's editors have been circumspect about revealing the scholars they consulted on the project, it is becoming increasingly clear that Baptist heavily influenced and likely advised Desmond's essay. Desmond essentially adopts *The Half Has Never Been Told* as the basis of his economic interpretation, and of the aforementioned statistics. It therefore casually repeats Baptist's errors and misrepresentations of Olmstead and Rhode's work.

Olmstead and Rhode's critique of Baptist falls squarely among the highest-profile academic debates of the last decade. In 2016 it broke away from the confines of academic journals and into mainstream journalism, with even the *Washington Post* running an essay on the dispute.[68]

Curiously, the 1619 Project's editors appear to have completely missed this dispute. When I asked her about Desmond's over-reliance on Ed Baptist's debunked claims, project editor Nikole Hannah-Jones responded, "Economists dispute a few of Baptist's calculations but not the book itself nor its thesis."[69]

Olmstead offers a very different assessment: "Edward Baptist's study of capitalism and slavery is flawed beyond repair."[70] And as we've now seen, Desmond's 1619 Project essay lifted its main empirical argument from Baptist and grafted it onto a false genealogy that

....

68 Jan, Tracy. 2016. "There's a bitter new battle over slave torture was the foundation fo the American economy." The Washington Post, December 12.

69 Hannah-Jones, Nikole. 2019. "Economists dispute a few of Baptist;s calculations but not the book itself nor its thesis." Twitter, August 18, 2019. https://twitter.com/nhannahjones/status/1163030801778401281

70 Murray, J., Olmstead, A., Logan, T., Pritchett, J., & Rousseau, P. 2015. "Roundtable of Reviews for 'The Half Has Never Been Told: Slavery and the Making of American Capitalism' By Edward E. Baptist." The Journal of Economic History, 75(03): 919-931.

purports to derive modern accounting practices from lineal "roots" in the plantation system.

It would seem, too, that Desmond's essay is flawed beyond repair.

As the *New York Times* often presents itself as a stickler for corrections in the name of ensuring factual and interpretive accuracy, substantial portions of Desmond's essay warrant retraction—including its main thesis linking modern capitalism to slavery.

A Comment on the 'New' History of American Capitalism

This longer paper, adapted from my published work on the subject, contains a historiographic discussion of the New History of Capitalism (NHC) literature. This emergent genre of historical scholarship forms the basis of Matthew Desmond's essay and argument. In my paper, I discuss the problems of the NHC literature, including its use of defective definitions for the term "capitalism" and its embrace of a heavily anti-capitalistic ideological lens.

* * *

Over half a century has passed since F. A. Hayek called attention to an "emotional aversion to 'capitalism'" within the history profession. He traced this criticism to a persistent belief that the industrial-competitive mechanisms of the modern era reached a sustained and unprecedented state of economic expansion at the expense of society's weakest members. If the economic enrichment since the industrial revolution was achieved on the backs of the poor, the economically ravaged, and the exploited, it is but a short step to brush aside the empirically attested abundance of 'capitalism' as a tainted good. Both then and now, such zero sum thinking depends upon an almost intentional myopia that constructs its evidence selectively to fit its already-accepted diagnosis of capitalism's ills. Yet its persistence constitutes the "one supreme myth which more than any other has served to discredit the economic system to which we owe our present-day civilization".[71] Perceptions of the past—including mistaken ones—are a heavy epistemic weight upon policy decisions in the present.

Simultaneously alarming and prescient, Hayek's description still rings true on many counts. Inequality in particular retains a persistent place in historical treatments of economic events, including a tendency to view the allocation of society's wealth as an end unto itself, or as a destabilizing causal mechanism behind a multitude of other social ills, as opposed to a measurement of other factors of growth and fiscal policy. While the topic is itself unobjectionable and even a necessary tool for assessing the distributional effects of economic outcomes, the historical study of inequality is almost always paired with prescriptive political arguments for redistributive policy making or vindications of past examples of the same.[72]

The history profession's attention shifted away from economic

....

71 Hayek, Friedrich A. 1954. *Capitalism and the Historians*, pp. 9-10. Chicago: University of Chicago Press.

72 For recent examples of inequality research that received both praise by historians and attention for their prescriptive calls for redistributive taxation, see Saez, Emmanuel, and Gabriel Zucman. 2014. "Exploding wealth inequality in the United States. *Washington, DC: Washington Center for Equitable Growth*, October 20; Piketty, Thomas. 2014. *Capital in the 21ˢᵗ Century*. Cambridge: Harvard University Press.

history in the second half of the 20th century, ceding this turf to an increasingly quantitative economic history subfield housed in economics departments. Mainstream historical interest in economic matters resurged with a vengeance following the financial crisis of 2008. The product is a loosely defined assemblage of economically themed research, sometimes referred to as the "New History of Capitalism" (NHC).[73] Although branded with the moniker "new," a number of its defining elements are not all that novel. While it would be a mistake to attribute ideological uniformity to this growing subfield, the core characteristics of Hayek's half-century-old diagnosis are abundant in this recent body of literature. Several leading works of NHC scholarship approach "capitalism" as a cohesive societal order or system, and an eminently blameworthy one at that. Themes of physical expropriation, distributional inequality, labor mistreatment, and economic exploitation linger in the background of much of this work, and—perhaps above all other concerns—attempts to causally link slavery to the emergence of a capitalist economic "system" are particularly strong.

In doing so, the distinctive feature of the NHC genre is not actually its claimed revival of a neglected set of topics that never really left the discussion. Historians have long studied questions of economic inequality and distribution, and the socio-economic dimensions of slavery have been a pre-eminent focus of historical attention for decades. Rather, what distinguishes recent works under the NHC moniker is their aggressive embrace of what Hayek diagnosed over half a century ago as a latent bias of academic historians. In attempting to

....

73 Schuessler, Jennifer. 2013. "In History Departments, It's Up With Capitalism." New York Times, April 6; Adelman, Jeremy and Jonathan Levy. 2014. "The Fall and Rise of Economic History." Chronicle of Higher Education, December 1.

study "capitalism," these works often begin from aggressively anti-capitalistic priors and peddle in the practice of infusing their authors' own ideological distastes for "capitalism," often broadly construed yet poorly defined, to long-familiar topics of historical study.

The tensions between NHC and classical liberalism are numerous and warrant consideration in detail, though one general development since Hayek's time suggests that capitalism's defenders enjoy an improved scholarly position in the present day even as the growth of the NHC movement portends invigorated hostilities. The intervening decades have yielded a vibrant scholarly literature on what Deirdre McCloskey has termed the "Great Enrichment"—the historically unparalleled expansion in the wealth and well-being of ordinary human lives that has occurred since roughly 1800. The attributed causes of this process are multifaceted and sometimes in tension with each other, though its major characteristics are situated somewhere between an emerging ethical and cultural valuation of economic production in the late 18th century, the existence of favorable legal and institutional characteristics, the improved access to and dissemination of requisite knowledge for productive processes, and the broader influence of the enlightenment upon the intellectual environment of the early industrial revolution.[74] Each offers a plausible interpretation of what might be

....

74 See in particular North, Douglass C. and Robert Paul Thomas. 1973. *The Rise of the Western World: A new economic history.* New York: Cambridge University Press; Mokyr, Joel. 2002. *The Gifts of Athena: Historical origins of the knowledge economy.* Princeton: Princeton University Press; Mokyr, Joel. 2009. *The Enlightened Economy: An Economic History of Britain 1700-1850.* New Haven: Yale University Press; McCloskey, Deirdre N. 2006. *Bourgeois Virtue.* John Wiley & Sons, Ltd.; McCloskey, Deirdre N. 2010. *Bourgeois Dignity: Why economics can't explain the modern world.* Chicago: University of Chicago Press.

called a capitalist age, for lack of a better term, rejecting the zero-sum disposition of recent NHC contributions and calling our attention to its empirically undeniable abundance.

A distinctive characteristic of the history of the "Great Enrichment" is its natural interaction with a number of classical liberal insights, particularly from economics. Its story rests upon an empirical observation of rapidly improved human well-being and attempts to discern its causal mechanisms not from any narrative plan or singular ideology, but through spontaneously organized exchange in a favorable cultural and institutional environment. Its story is not premised upon an idealized conception of "capitalism" or the denial of historical experiences in its wake, injustices among them, but rather the humility to ask whether such a diverse array of events can be legitimately ascribed to a single system.

Capitalism was not proclaimed, adopted, imposed, or arrived at as a moment in time. In the classical liberal sense, capitalism simply refers to a set of conditions and circumstances that are favorable to voluntary human interactions and that are distinguished by their absence of a centralized design. It describes a number of attributes in an economy—a freedom in the exchange and movement of goods and people, a general recognition of the validity of private property and a stable and discernable system of contracts built upon it, a cultural environment of toleration for choice and celebration of discovery, and a worldview that—at least in its professed values—deprecates forceful predation, whether by other economic actors or the power of the nation-state. A classical liberal history of capitalism is therefore a history of the conditions that permit free exchange and discovery, and with them the witnessed results of the past two hundred years.

The divergence between this conceptualization and the emerging NHC literature is profound. It presents two distinctive stories: a classical liberal capitalism as a descriptive term for spontaneously ordering interactions of the past, and an ideological capitalism that quite literally serves as a lightning rod for faults and blame in interpreting the past's many ills. What follows in this discussion is a brief examination of some of the main features and themes of the NHC literature and its tensions with the former classical liberal conceptualization. What this framing portends for the historical discussion of capitalism remains to be seen, and will likely attract much scholarly attention in the coming years. As this discussion will highlight, many of the differences between the two approaches stem from a disciplinary divide between historians and economists. One consequence of this divide may be seen in a number of profound methodological and definitional imprecisions afflicting the recent NHC genre, setting up the conditions in which strong ideological priors have become a primary motive for this line of research.

Between Divergent Paths

The study of history in the latter part of the 20th century was distinguished by a methodological divide between an older approach rooted in evidentiary empiricism and an emergent attention to social history, and particularly that of group identities based on racial, class, and gender lines. Few subfields were more directly affected by this divide than economic history. Once an inter-disciplinary domain that attracted collaborative conversations between economists and historians, the subfield was largely swept up in the "cliometric revolution" that took hold in the early 1960s. In some sense an extreme form of quantitative empiricism in its own right, the cliometric approach saw the emerging tools of statistics, econometrics, and economic modeling applied to historical analysis. Social history in turn pulled the attention of many traditional historians away from an ever-specialized discussion of economic matters, albeit with occasional forays on a topic by topic basis. Slavery was one such example where the methodological pathways between economics and historians diverged sharply.[75]

Some of the earliest cliometric work applied heavy data analysis to the ever-topical economic question of slavery's economics, and particularly its profitability. The economic theories of a century prior had conventionally asserted an intuitive tension between slavery and capitalism premised on free labor. In addition to its moral dimensions, slavery removed the economic incentive of the slave to better his product and introduced a number of inefficiencies to its productive processes—particularly those measured in lost opportunity.[76] The empirical investigation of slavery's profitability in the second half of the 20th century shifted this discussion. While the new empirical literature did not establish slavery's immunity from the economic inefficiencies with which it had been charged, and sometimes punted on this question entirely, it did show the economic viability of plantation production in the late antebellum. The economists, it seems, had uncovered a reason

....

75 An interesting assessment of the opinions of economic historians on slavery and a number of other issues may be found in Whaples, Robert. 1995. "Where is there consensus among American economic historians? The results of a survey on forty propositions." *The Journal of Economic History,* 55(01), 139-154; For a review of the literature on slavery, profitability, and the divisions between historians and economists, see Hummel, Jeffrey Rogers. 2012. Chapter 1. In *Deadweight Loss and the American Civil War: The Political Economy of Slavery, Secession, and Emancipation.* October 1.

76 Several abolitionist works advanced this notion as a critique of slavery on the eve of the Civil War. See Atkinson, Edward. 1861. *Cheap Cotton by Free Labor.* A. Williams Publisher; Olmsted, Frederick Law and Arthur Meier Schlesinger. 1996. *The Cotton Kingdom: A Traveller's Observations on Cotton and Slavery in the American Slave States: Based Upon Three Former Volumes of Journeys and Investigations by the Same Author.* Da Capo Press.

in profitability that explained slavery's persistence. The evidence, at least on that point, ran counter to a somewhat wishful 19th century belief among some abolition-minded economists that the plantation system, if left to its own devices, would be outcompeted and die a natural death.

In a sense, the study of the economic dimensions of slavery are a microcosm for the subsequent compartmentalization of economic history onto divergent trajectories.[77] The cliometric end of this genre peaked with Robert Fogel and Stanley Engerman's landmark *Time on the Cross* in 1973, notable for the outpouring of respondents it provoked among historians and economists alike as well as its controversial but data-driven substantiation of the plantation system's profitability. This last point instigated something of a sea change in economic history, as it ran counter to both elements of an existing historical literature on slavery and the aforementioned conventional assumptions of economic thought about slave labor in the 19th century. Curiously, the ensuing debate over slavery's profitability—and with it an oft-implied but sometimes contested claim of slavery's economic efficiency—was never quite settled, though conflicting claims of victory persist among the cliometric economists and traditional historians alike.[78]

It is likely no coincidence that the slave economy is a central focus

....

77 Conrad, Alfred H. and John R. Meyer. 1958. "The economics of slavery in the ante bellum South." *The Journal of Political Economy,* 95-130; North, Douglas 1965. "The State of Economic History." *American Economic Review.* 55 (1–2), 86–91; Fogel, Robert William and Stanley L. Engerman. 1995. *Time on the cross: The economics of American Negro slavery.* Vol. 1. WW Norton & Company. See also Hummel (2012, Introduction and Chapter 1).

78 Hummel (2012, Introduction).

of NHC scholarship.[79] The causal relationships implied by much of this literature are remarkably fluid, such that capitalism is simultaneously an enabling prerequisite of large-scale (and race-based) plantation slavery, as distinct from the ancient world institution, as well as its most visible beneficiary—an economic system propelled to modernity upon the backs of the slaves. In either case, many NHC scholars advance a politically tinged subtext that effectively saddles capitalism with both cause and credit for slavery's economic output and therefore, by implication, its moral price tag.

The themes of these contributions differ somewhat, with emphases that range from tracing the global reach and economic uses of plantation-derived products to the specific labor practices that were deployed to extract production from enslaved persons. The method of analysis is largely rooted in social observation and an archive-sustained story. Market wide data interpretation takes a back seat to multi-method narrative. At its best, historical work of this type teases observations about slavery's production from the stories of individual plantations and shippers, the testimonies of former slaves where they exist, and the descriptive indicators of life on the plantation. The economic reach of slavery's output and other plantation-linked activities in shipping, finance, and production thus become the evidence of slavery's own centrality to the economic system in which it operated.

....

79 See in particular Johnson, Walter. 2013. *River of Dark Dreams*. Cambridge: Harvard University Press; Baptist, Edward E. 2014. *The Half Has Never Been Told: Slavery and the Making of American Capitalism*. New York: Basic Books; Beckert, Sven. 2015. *Empire of cotton: A global history*. Vintage; Schermerhorn, Calvin. 2015. *The Business of Slavery and the Rise of American Capitalism*, 1815-1860. New Haven: Yale University Press; Beckert, Sven and Seth Rockman. 2016. *Slavery's Capitalism: A New History of American Economic Development*. Philadelphia: University of Pennsylvania Press.

Despite methodological differences in assembling its evidence and interpreting its findings, a recurring feature of the NHC literature is that it arrives at one strikingly similar position as the economists. Both largely agree on slavery's profitability.[80] And both advance a rejection of at least the simplified forms of the older classical economic—and, to some degree, classical liberal—conclusion that slavery was unsuited for industrial capitalism on account of its comparative inefficiency to free labor.

It is all the more curious that several primary works of the NHC literature in the last five years appear to be only nominally aware of, or at least inattentive to, the discussions surrounding older cliometric and derivative economic investigations of the same topic, even where they drifted into the debates of the mainstream history profession in the 1970s and 80s.

To the contrary, much of the NHC work on slavery seems to be enamored with its own claims of novelty—of telling a "never told" story that has in fact appeared many times before, and that even bears a striking resemblance to the old "King Cotton" arguments that were advanced by pro-slavery radicals and Confederate nationalists in the 19th century. Consider the following excerpt from an 1856 tract:[81]

> "Slavery is not an isolated system, but is so mingled with the business of the world, that it derives facilities from the most innocent transactions. Capital and labor, in Europe and America,

....

80 Whaples (1995).

81 Christy, David. (1856). Chapter V. In *Cotton is King: Or, The Culture of Cotton, and Its Relation to Agriculture, Manufactures and Commerce*; and *Also to the Free Colored People*; and to *Those who Hold that Slavery is in Itself Sinful*. New York, NY. Derby & Jackson.

are largely employed in the manufacture of cotton. These goods, to a great extent, may be seen freighting every vessel, from Christian nations, that traverses the seas of the globe; and filling the warehouses and shelves of the merchants over two-thirds of the world. By the industry, skill, and enterprise employed in the manufacture of cotton, mankind are better clothed; their comfort better promoted; general industry more highly stimulated; commerce more widely extended; and civilization more rapidly advanced than in any preceding age."

But for slight idiosyncrasies of tone and terminology, this cotton-centric accounting of global political economy at the middle of the 19th century could be mistaken for the primary arguments of NHC historians Sven Beckert and Edward Baptist. Beckert, for example, places a cotton-centric "war capitalism" that extends its reach into "insurance, finance, and shipping" as well as "public institutions such as government credit, money itself, and national defense." Baptist depicts a cotton-driven economic empire where slavery's reach drives everything from shipping, to "insurance and interest paid on commercial credit," to the "purchase of land, the cost of credit for such purchases, the pork and the corn bought at the river landings," to "money spent by millworkers and Illinois hog farmers, the wages paid to steamboat workers, and the revenues yielded by investments made with the profits of the merchants, manufacturers, and slave traders who derived some or all of their income either directly or indirectly from the southwestern fields" to the clothing and toolmakers who supplied the plantations to, of course, the vast sums of money invested in the slaves themselves.[82]

NHC scholars have not simply stumbled into a long-running debate about the efficiency of slave labor. They have also somewhat accidentally adopted an economic interpretation that finds its primary historical champions in the late antebellum bluster of James Henry Hammond, and the failed economic strategy of the Confederacy's diplomatic overtures to Europe.[83]

The ensuing NHC–cliometric divide has become pronounced and, at times, embittered.[84] Based on the sheer weight of evidence, the data driven economic historians have often gained the upper hand by highlighting basic errors of empirical interpretation. Economists Alan Olmstead and Paul Rhode severely chastised the NHC literature for misusing historical cotton production data, including statistics that were derived from their own work. In another revealing indicator of the divide, economist Bradley Hanson noted a basic conceptual

....

82 Beckert (2015, p. 52); Baptist (2015, pp. 321-22).

83 Speech of James H. Hammond 1858. *Congressional Globe*. 35th Congress, (1st Session, March 4): Appendix, p. 70. If the plantation system was as intractable from the global economy as the NHC literature claims, then the Confederacy's diplomatic strategy might have assured rapid intervention in the American Civil War from the European beneficiaries of its yield. As it happened, the strategy was largely a failure. Owsley, F. L. 1959. *King Cotton Diplomacy*. University of Alabama Press.

84 See in particular Parry, Marc. 2016. "Shackles and Dollars." *Chronicle of Higher Education*, December 8; Murray, J., Olmstead, A., Logan, T., Pritchett, J., & Rousseau, P. 2015. "Roundtable of Reviews for 'The Half Has Never Been Told: Slavery and the Making of American Capitalism' By Edward E. Baptist." *The Journal of Economic History,* 75(03): 919-931; Clegg, John J. 2015. "Capitalism and Slavery." *Critical Historical Studies,* 2(2): 281-304; Baptist, Edward E. 2015. "Correcting an Incorrect "Corrective"." *The Junto*, November 4; Olmstead, Alan L. and Paul W. Rhode. 2018. "Cotton, slavery, and the new history of capitalism." *Explorations in Economic History*, January.

misunderstanding in NHC scholar Edward Baptist's attempt to calculate the percentage of the antebellum United States' gross domestic product that derived from slavery. Unaware of basic national income accounting practices in differentiating input costs from final goods, Baptist inadvertently double- and perhaps triple-counted cotton-derived products until he reached an empirically unsupported figure that attributed nearly half of the United States' economic output in 1836 to plantation slavery.[85]

While episodes of this sort point to a specific shortcoming in the NHC literature, itself enabled by a predisposition toward "evidence" that appears to confirm a central link between slavery and capitalism, they also show the failure of even basic economic insights to penetrate the process of peer reviewing mainstream historical works that make economic claims. While it might be tempting to fault the confirmation biases of the historians' engagement with data, and the ideological undertones of their work suggests as much, another part of the problem derives from the methodological rift with the economists.

Cliometric research comes with a steep learning curve that can, at times, render its findings inaccessible to scholars who lack intensive training in advanced econometric techniques and statistical analysis. This obstacle extends well beyond the economics of slavery, leading to cases where parallel but divergent literatures emerge on either methodological divide of the same historical subject, largely in isolation from each other. For a simple illustration, consider the widespread enthusiasm that most historians show for Franklin Roosevelt's New Deal as an effective and necessary response to the Great Depression.

....

85 Olmstead and Rhode (2016); Hanson, Bradley A. 2014. "The Back of Ed Baptist's Envelope." October 30.

Almost unbeknownst to them, a parallel literature in economic history largely holds that many of these same policies as well as other lesser known "relief" measures inadvertently impeded recovery and likely prolonged the Great Depression.[86]

The divide often produces competing claimants to accuracy, even where less dissimilar positions result. Economists embrace data as a benchmark of social-scientific methods to test and validate specific claims about the past. The traditional historians in turn retort, with some validity, that the data-heavy modeling on the other side of the divide has its own limitations. For one, it can artificially constrain historical inquiry to topics where identifiable quantitative metrics exist. There are no serialized archives of the trade volume of the Ostrogothic Kingdom after all, though much else might be said about the economies of late antiquity and early medieval Europe from surviving manuscript sources and even archaeological evidence. Second, the overly cliometric emphasis of some economic history outlets often comes at the expense of the deep contextual detail that narrative historians utilize to interpret events—a point that Baptist has enlisted to his defense in the slavery debate.

These concerns are neither recent nor unfamiliar to the number crunchers of the economics profession's historical subfields. Some two decades ago, economic historian Avner Greif cautioned that the dominant framework of the neoclassical model is self-limiting in its

....

86 Friedman, Milton, and Anna Jacobson Schwartz. 2008. *A Monetary History of the United States, 1867-1960*. Princeton: Princeton University Press; Cole, Harold L. and Ohanian, Lee E. 2004. "New Deal policies and the persistence of the Great Depression: A general equilibrium analysis." *Journal of Political Economy* 112(4): 779-816; Higgs, Robert. 2006. Chapter 1. In *Depression, war, and cold war: Studies in political economy*. Oxford: Oxford University Press.

extension to historical events. In searching for markets to analyze, it imposes ahistorical theoretical assumptions about individual preferences, technology, factor endowments, and market institutions to historical events. Greif noted the effects of this emphasis upon economic history in the period since the cliometric revolution. It appeared in the neglect of "issues that were traditionally the focus of economic historians" before the emergence of quantitative dominance. Lost were historical inquiries into "the nature and role of non-market institutions, culture, entrepreneurship, technological and organizational innovation, politics, social factors, distributional conflicts, and the historical processes through which economies grew and declined."[87]

The persistence of the problem is highlighted in the recent resurgence of historical attention to these same topics, as seen in the NHC literature and parallel tracks. Yet the challenge we have witnessed is largely one of traditional historians who are steeped in contextual detail about economic events but ill-equipped to engage them with economic tools, hence Baptist's confusion-laden foray into national income accounting. The NHC literature at its worst accordingly becomes not a renewed exercise in qualitative economic history, but a somewhat haphazard misapplication of social history tools to the complex economic events of the past.

The resulting picture may seem mired in its inflexibility. On one side we find a self-limiting methodological rigidity that restricts its subject matter's accessibility to non-specialist audiences and self-limits the deployment of economic analysis to unconventional topics that are not easily quantified. On the other, we find a sea of abundant but cluttered

....

87 Greif, Avner. 1997. "Cliometrics after 40 years." *The American Economic Review*, 87(2): 400-403.

detail and endless direction, yet also one where the only vessels are navigating by picking out bits and pieces of flotsam based on their resemblance to a strong and imported ideological prior that largely distrusts market capitalism itself.

Curiously, the classical liberal historian may be uniquely situated to operate across the rift in the history of capitalism. The conceptual toolbox of thinking economically—of grounding oneself in the concepts of scarcity, of trade-offs, of incentives, and of institutional political economy—provides an interpretive grounding that addresses the limitations of both sides. What might we find when we examine the effects of the institutional constraints of constitutions, the robustness of private property, and the conflict-adjudicating mechanisms of a legal system upon the economic events of the past? What happens when historical actors are scrutinized for their susceptibility to the same patterns of political economy that we witness among state actors in the present? How well do historical economic events since 1776 comport to or break from the original Smithian project of finding the underlying nature and causes of the wealth of nations? In short, a classical liberal approach to the history of capitalism might consider taking economic insights to topics that exist beyond the methodological barriers of cliometrics and yet are also neglected, or worse erroneously serviced, by historians who lack or even eschew and caricature economic intuition.

Slavery and Capitalism: Friend or Foe?

Despite enjoying a common and in some ways concurrent intellectual history with the emergence of capitalism, a classical liberal history of capitalism must also grapple with a related ailment of its subject's historical treatment that has become increasingly pronounced since the in recent years. Capitalism suffers from a definitional problem. While the persistence of market-hostile ideological frameworks in historical scholarship is in some ways a culprit, it is also the case that these new historians of "capitalism" simply lack a cohesive definition of the term and stumble from there into imprecision. The worst instances devolve into a dereliction of meaning itself, with the usage of the term "capitalism" taking on an almost intentionally pejorative character in the absence of anything more substantive.

A number of scholars have commented upon the pronounced "definitional elasticity" of recent historical work on capitalism, particularly within the NHC literature. Several NHC practitioners have in turn embraced this reluctance to define the term as a virtue of their approach. To quote NHC historian Seth Rockman, this line of study "has minimal investment in a fixed or theoretical definition of capitalism." Characterizing his approach as a process of inductive discovery, he openly concedes a willingness to let the term "float as a placeholder." Rockman further promotes a "capitalism" that is loosened from its conventional association with specific eras such as the industrial revolution, obviating questions of a pre-capitalist society or its causal role in transitions from an earlier state.[88] Louis Hyman echoes these sentiments even more forcefully in a recent *Journal of American History* roundtable on the subject: "Simply defining capitalism is a bad idea. It is too deductive."[89]

This curious state of affairs has received some pushback from other historians. In the same roundtable discussion, Scott Marler suggested

....

88 Rockman, Seth. 2014. "What Makes the History of Capitalism Newsworthy?" *Journal of the Early Republic,* 34(3): 442.

89 Beckert, Sven, Angus Burgin, Peter James Hudson, Louis Hyman, Naomi Lamoreaus, Scott Marler, Stephen Mihm, Julia Ott, Philip Scranton and Elizabeth Tandy Shermer. 2014. "Interchange: The History of Capitalism." *Journal of American History,* 101(2): 503-36.

this aversion to a definition was self-defeating in that it shirked an admittedly complex but historiographically important question. Tom Cutterham similarly criticized the "rather troubling" implications of Rockman's aversion to definitions precisely because they strip capitalism of its grounding in time. "If there was no transition to capitalism, if nothing can properly be called pre-capitalist, then has it simply always been here?" he asks. The result is to turn capitalism into an overly broad term, wherein it becomes impossible to "point to anything that was ever not capitalism."[90]

The NHC struggles with an adequate definition of capitalism creates additional oddities, including contradicting its own claimed premise. Instead of inductively teasing out the historical mechanisms of capitalism, these definition-averse historians have created the conditions of a never-ending cycle of "discovering" something that is never quite fully revealed or specified.

Far more problematic though is a second and less-noticed implication of adopting an intentionally vague terminology. Even while claiming to eschew definitions of "capitalism," many of these same historians have in fact imported a certain semiotic fluidity to their deployment of the term. The result is not only to broaden its meaning, but to do so selectively and in ways that are vulnerable to the importation of intentionally disparaging characteristics.

Consider Rockman's example. In the very same sentence he touts the "disavowal of theoretical definitions" of capitalism as a necessary feature of its open inquiry, he announces quite confidently that NHC scholarship has shown "slavery as integral, rather than oppositional, to

....

90 Cutterham, Tom. 2014. "Is the History of Capitalism the History of Every-thing?" *The Junto*, September 2.

capitalism."[91] One cannot specify the characteristics of capitalism for even modest conceptual clarity, and yet slavery is already admitted as an integral characteristic of capitalism. A rather awkward doctrine, this!

Internally conflicted assessments of this type are not limited to Rockman. NHC historian Sven Beckert is even more brash in his assault on "capitalism's illiberal origins." At once evading a definition for capitalism and yet aggressively infusing it with specific—and damning—attributes, he pinpoints slavery as the "beating heart of this new system"—a system built not on property rights "but a wave of expropriation of labor and land."[92] Beckert too is quite certain that capitalism and slavery are not oppositional. Or as he approvingly paraphrases Walter Johnson's parallel argument in *River of Dark Dreams*, "slavery [is] not just as an integral part of American capitalism, but... its very essence."[93]

Issues of definitional rigor and consistency extend deep within the NHC literature, and Beckert offers his own addendum. By little more than reinventing terminology, he blends the attributes of 18th century imperial mercantilism—that aggressively managed symbiosis of economic interests and nationally-minded state policies to drive expansion and industry—into market capitalism under the new moniker "war capitalism" and proceeds as if the two are unified, both in character and culpability for slavery and a host of other ills.[94] The pronounced adversarial tension that historically existed between market capitalism

....

91 Rockman (2014, p. 444).

92 Beckert, *Empire of Cotton* (2014, p. 37).

93 Beckert, Sven. 2014. "Slavery and Capitalism". *Chronicle of Higher Education*, December 12.

94 Beckert, *Empire of Cotton* (2014, p. xvi).

and the mercantile political agenda is almost entirely lost in the process, even as the past's participants in the intellectual contests between them would have balked at any attempt to blend the two together.

The abusiveness of the historical distortion exhibited in Beckert's move is no small point. It inverts the very premise of capitalism's most famous and influential exposition. Composed as a retort to the prevailing mercantilist economic theories of his day, Adam Smith's *Wealth of Nations* was also a far-reaching assault upon industrial protectionism in the name of national "wealth," upon public-private enterprises undertaken through the privileged arrangements of law and government access, upon militaristic imperialism and colonialism, and upon slavery itself.[95] Beckert's version of "capitalism," still wavering between a definition that is at once equivocal in its characteristics and yet selectively infused with the certitude of an "essence" chained to slavery, has effectively become the same horde of demons that the primary intellectual father of modern capitalism specifically contested and condemned in his seminal work.

Nor is Beckert anomalous in this practice. Johnson similarly invents the phrase "racial slave capitalism" to describe a program of white supremacist mercantile internationalism. The features of this "system" unite agriculture and industry around the steam transport of cotton through a vast and globally minded system of state collusion and a vigorously regulated color bar.[96] The resulting concoction is simultaneously part Friedrich List, part Henry Clay, part J.D.B. DeBow, and

....

95 See in particular: Smith, Adam. 1776. Book III, Chapter II and Book IV, Chapter VIII. In *An Inquiry into the Nature and Causes of the Wealth of Nations*.

96 Johnson (2013, p. 14).

part George Fitzhugh, yet few of its ingredients are quintessentially capitalistic in the Smithian sense and many are explicitly antithetical. A large economic literature empirically establishes and expands upon the economic costs of a discriminatory legal regime, as well as the tendency of market forces to rub against statutorily entrenched racial codes.[97] Smith himself saw this tension at play in slavery, observing that the entire system was sustained upon the political assistance its beneficiaries afforded to themselves. Thus the slave-owners "will never make any laws mitigating their usage; whatever laws are made with regard to slaves are intended to strengthen the authority of the masters and reduce the slaves to a more absolute subjection."[98]

This specific criticism is not offered to suggest that Smith retains a perpetual license upon determining the attributes of the economic system he described. Even the term's acquisition of its modern properties postdates his lifespan. Yet the pronounced dissimilarities between Smithian capitalism and what the NHC literature takes to be its subject matter point to another opportunity for classical liberal historians to unclutter the discussion. A history of capitalism attempted without the benefit of an intellectual history of capitalism arrives in strange and even self-contradictory positions, among them the odd state of affairs where capitalism becomes, by little more than a sleight of hand and twist in terminology, the very same practices of 18th century political economy that Adam Smith and the other celebrated theorists of capitalism specifically argued against.

....

97 Becker, Gary S. 1957. *The economics of discrimination.* Chicago: University of Chicago Press; Hutt, William H. 1964. *Economics of the Colour Bar.* London: Institute of Economic Affairs.

98 Smith, Adam. 1982. "Lectures on Jurisprudence." Liberty Fund, p. 181.

Anti-Capitalism as a Historical Method

There appears to be another twist at play in the definitional fluidity of the NHC, and it is here that the old Hayekian criticism's application to the modern literature becomes most salient. While selectively non-committal phrasings and ahistorical inversions of terminology can serve as a mechanism to insulate a claim about the past from the sort of falsifiable testing that economic historians prefer, they also contrast with a consistent theme of the NHC genre found in its recurring portrayal of capitalism as an explicitly illiberal system, or one of uncontested illiberal byproducts. Beckert openly states as much in asserting the "illiberal origins" of modern market capitalism, and the larger NHC genre exhibits an almost singular preoccupation with forging a friendship between capitalism and slavery; and segregation; and colonialism; and exploitation, degradation, and violence, all chalked up to "market failure" or worse.[99] For all these attempts to forge—and force—an association between capitalism and a multitude of social wrongs and problems, a parallel neglect extends to the historical critics of capitalism as they saw the Smithian system unfolding in the world around them.

Seeing the now-disputed adversarial economic relationship between capitalism and slavery, many classical economists in the 18th and 19th centuries openly advanced abolitionist arguments in their works.[100] Less noticed as a historical point however is the frequency with which their contemporary advocates of economic regulation, of planned economic nationalism, and even slavery itself also perceived capitalism as a

....

99 Beckert, *Empire of Cotton,* 2014, p. 37

100 Atkinson (1861); Cairnes, John E. 1862. *The Slave Power: Its Character, Career, and Probable Designs.* New York.

threat. A number of these anti-capitalist witnesses are noteworthy not only for their defenses of illiberal institutions and practices, but also as forbearers of many of the same arguments against unchained markets—against the much-caricatured capitalist notion of laissez-faire—that persist to the present day.

Consider the case of Thomas Carlyle, the Scottish historian and social commentator who penned a now-notorious essay that blamed the economic decline of the British West Indies on emancipation. His 1849 lamentation took direct aim at what he famously dubbed the "dismal science"—a "rueful" enterprise "which finds the secret of this universe in "supply and demand," and reduces the duty of human governors to that of letting men alone," which is to say laissez-faire. To Carlyle, this new science of economy had joined itself to the "sacred cause of black emancipation, or the like, to fall in love and make a wedding of it" to yield "dark extensive moon-calves, unnameable abortions, wide-coiled monstrosities, such as the world has not seen hitherto."[101]

This bombastic slur was no passing criticism, but rather a sustained assault on market capitalism. Carlyle saw cause for alarm in the "multifarious devices we have been endeavoring to dispense with governing" in deference to markets where the two collided. He denounced the "superficial speculations, of laissez-faire, supply-and-demand" not only in its affinity for emancipation, but as a blamed cause for other ills of the day—for the Irish famine, as he extended his doctrines in the immediate wake of the 1849 essay.[102] In two decades' time,

....

101 Carlyle, Thomas. 1849. "Occasional Discourse on the Negro Question." Frasers Magazine for Town and Country, February. See also Levy, David M. 2002. How the Dismal Science got its Name: Classical economics and the ur-text of racial politics. Ann Arbor: University of Michigan Press.

102 Carlyle, Thomas. 1850. *Latter Day Pamphlets*. London: Chapman & Hall, p. 34.

with abolition achieved not only in Britain's colonies but the United States, he placed market capitalism at the center of blame for a society "fallen vulgar and chaotic" to the simultaneous forces of black equality and "cheap and nasty"—his term for an over-commodified marketplace of unimpeded trade and what he saw as culturally-degrading commercialism.[103]

A parallel witness may be seen in the previously referenced late antebellum theorist of the slaveocracy, George Fitzhugh. A self-described Carlylean, Fitzhugh was also an avowed anti-capitalist. Political economy, which "may be summed up in the phrase, 'Laissez-faire,' or 'Let alone'" was but a "false philosophy of the age."[104] These principles, he asserted in another text, "are at war with all kinds of slavery." Capitalism represented a competitive race to the bottom of wages in Fitzhugh's mind, and slavery was its well-ordered antithesis. Yet slavery was not Fitzhugh's only concern. He devoted chapters in both of his major works to lambasting the cause of free trade. Its intellectual champion Adam Smith was, to him, an "absent, secluded and unobservant" thinker who "saw only that prosperous and progressive portion of society whom liberty or free competition benefitted, and mistook its effects on them for its effects on the world." Just as revealing is Fitzhugh's antidote to this perceived state of affairs:[105]

....

103 Carlyle, Thomas. 1867. *Shooting Niagara: And After?* London: Chapman and Hall.

104 Fitzhugh, George. 1857. *Cannibals All! Or, Slaves Without Masters* (electronic ed.), p. 79. Richmond: A. Morris, Publisher. https://docsouth.unc.edu/southlit/fitzhughcan/fitzcan.html

105 Fitzhugh, George. 1854. *Sociology for the South Or The Failure of Free Society* (electronic ed.). Richmond: A. Morris, Publisher. https://docsouth.unc.edu/southlit/fitzhughsoc/fitzhugh.html. At pp. 7, 10, 188.

But [the South] does not let alone. She builds roads and canals, encourages education, endows schools and colleges, improves river navigation, excludes, or taxes heavily foreign show-men, foreign pedlars, sellers of clocks, etc. tries to build up by legislation Southern commerce, and by State legislation to multiply and encourage industrial pursuits. Protection by the State Government is her established policy - and that is the only expedient or constitutional protection. It is time for her to avow her change of policy and opinion, and to throw Adam Smith, Say, Ricardo & Co., in the fire.

Fitzhugh's political recommendation is, with no small irony, strikingly similar to the managerial mercantile platform that the NHC literature rebrands as "war capitalism" or "slave capitalism." Beckert offers a parallel rejection of "liberal, lean state" 19th century Britain, depicting instead a slavery-fed plantation and cotton-driven "capitalist" empire with "a powerful and interventionist bureaucracy, high taxes, skyrocketing government debt, and protectionist tariffs," with "turnpikes and canals," and with conscious state policies to drive economic growth.[106] While the NHC literature diverges sharply from Fitzhugh in condemning the viciousness of slavery, its representation of the slave economy largely shares and emphasizes these same features: an assertion of the plantation system's economic prowess and dynamism, as distinct from classical economic criticisms that saw it as an inefficient and institutionally rigid throwback, and a mutual identification of slavery as the primary driving engine of economic industrialization taking place around it and in its wake. Fitzhugh also

....

106 Beckert (2015, pp. xv, 78).

differs by including a more candid admission about his own adversaries. They are one and the same with the capitalist intellectuals that much of the NHC literature now carelessly lumps into an extension of Fitzhugh's slave-based economic system.

Anti-Capitalism and Progressive History

Carlyle's influence and reputation have diminished since his lifetime, and Fitzhugh was always considered something of a crank beyond the fire-eaters of the slave-owning political class. Parallel manifestations of anti-capitalism nonetheless transmitted into subsequent intellectual movements at the root of American progressivism.

To some degree, the modern roots of anti-capitalistic historical writing are products of intellectual histories about older theorists of capitalism. Richard Hofstadter's classic 1944 assault on the claimed "social Darwinism" of Herbert Spencer and other laissez-faire theorists of the late 19th century still looms large in the history profession's conceptualization of pre- progressive-era models of capitalism. Hofstadter's text is not without flaws as more recent works on Spencer have suggested, but neither is it without nuance. At points he takes a more progressive strain of "Darwinian collectivism" to task even as the thrust of his work targets the "individualist" varieties of laissez-faire capitalism.[107] A curious feature of the more recent historical literature is that it retains Hofstadter's disapproving depictions of

....

107 Leonard, Thomas C. 2009. "Origins of the myth of social Darwinism: The ambiguous legacy of Richard Hofstadter's Social Darwinism in American Thought." *Journal of Economic Behavior & Organization,* 71(1): 37-51; Zwolinski, Matt. 2015. "Social Darwinism and Social Justice: Herbert Spencer on Our Duties to the Poor.*" Distributive Justice Debates in Social and Political Thought: Perspectives on Finding A Fair Share.* April 13. Routledge Publishing.

Spencerian laissez-faire capitalism and inflates them to the point of caricature, placing them at the source of historical racism, exploitation theory, and most pre-welfare state social ills. At the same time though, a profound inattention may be observed in parallel treatments of progressive economic causes that resonate among anti-capitalists despite carrying profoundly illiberal racial and social baggage in their respective histories.

One noteworthy expression appeared among a group of politically progressive economists in the late 19th and early 20th century who consciously set out to supplant economic non-intervention with "scientific" correctives that aimed to alleviate a host of economic ills attributed to low wages and unemployment, distributional inequality, and regulatory laxity. This outwardly progressive counter to laissez-faire coalesced in the late 19th century around a group of economists and other social scientists who shared common intellectual roots, many of them having trained under the "younger" German Historical School at the Universities of Halle and Heidelberg. Though a new infusion to the classical-aligned American economics scene of the 1880s, these progressive reformers could trace their intellectual lineage back to the older neo-mercantile political economy of Alexander Hamilton and its subsequent transmission to Germany in the early decades of the century.[108] The progressives used their academic work to advance a broad range of reformist causes, including labor unionization, work hour regulations, product safety regulations, anti-monopoly laws and trust-busting, "scientific" tariff targeting for strategic industries,

....

108 For a related history of both Hamilton's transmission to the German Historical School, and its continued influence upon the historical profession see Eicholz, Hans L. 2014. "Hamilton, Harvard, and the German Historical School: A Short Note on a Curious History." *Journal of Private Enterprise,* 29(3): 43.

redistributive taxation, and even the minimum wage. At the root of the movement was a widespread belief in the deployment of "scientific" managerial expertise to advise and design policies in areas where the unfettered free market fell short—where capitalism "failed" in their eyes.

The underlying rationale of progressive era economics is not far removed from similar progressive causes of today, including those championed by modern historian-advocates who are often drawn to these historical topics by political affinities and their own areas of interest. Indeed, the same NHC literature that condemns capitalism for an "integral" relationship with slavery a generation prior appears to hold the turn-of-the-century progressive rejoinder to laissez-faire in consistently high esteem. It entails a comparatively less developed body of work, though the thrust is highly approving of the progressive economic positions advanced by these historical figures.[109] Topically, there is little new to it save the investigation of unturned detail. The historiographical habit of portraying the progressive era as a corrective to the "excesses" of the Gilded Age is as old as it is oversimplified, yet it is also finding a comfortable embrace in recent NHC work.

The political economy of the progressive era warrants mention though for the complication it reveals, both historically among an identifiable group of capitalism's critics and in the present among historians who openly align with the causes they championed. Progressive scientism led its practitioners in a number of less-enlightened directions that are also just beginning to receive historical scrutiny.

....

109 Recent examples include Mehrotra, Ajay K. 2013. *Making the Modern American Fiscal State: Law, Politics, and the Rise of Progressive Taxation, 1877-1929*. Cambridge University Press; Fink, Leon. 2014. *The Long Gilded Age: American Capitalism and the Lessons of a New World Order*. Philadelphia: University of Pennsylvania Press.

The product shows a selectivity of blame in the larger attempt to link capitalism to slavery's illiberal terms, juxtaposed against a polite inattention that sets in with issues that reflect poorly upon the liberality of progressive causes.

Classical liberal engagement with the history of capitalism should note the illiberal dimensions of progressivism in a growing body of recent work on the downsides of "scientific" planning. The same mindset that prompted the progressives to enlist state tools to counter the perceived "market failures" also saw, and for parallel rationales, an aggressive role for the state in the correction of other perceived social ills. Progressivism's faults extend directly into the realm of eugenics, of forced sterilization of the "unfit," and of an assortment of pseudo-scientific theories of racial biology and psychology. They include the use of minimum wage laws and work hour regulations to exclude black and immigrant laborers from the turn-of-the-century workforce. They include racially discriminatory and pseudo-scientific drug policies, the legacies of which persist in the prison system of our own time. They also show numerous instances where the segregationist strictures of Jim Crow found a welcome partnership not in capitalism, but among its critics and "reformers." Some of the figures are relatively obscure—Richard T. Ely, John R. Commons, and Simon N. Patten to name a few.[110] Others like Woodrow Wilson are well known for infusing progressivism into mainstream political economy into the present day, again on terms that sought to correct capitalism's claimed defects.

....

110 Leonard, Thomas C. 2003. "'More Merciful and Not Less Effective': Eugenics and American Economics in the Progressive Era." *History of Political Economy* 35(4): 687-712; Leonard, Thomas C. 2016. *Illiberal Reformers: Race, Eugenics, and American Economics in the Progressive Era.* Princeton: Princeton University Press.

No less a source than John Maynard Keynes developed his original attack on market failure upon a eugenic argument for population controls. The "laissez-faire" of nature and heredity was, to him, as problematic as taking the same approach to an unregulated economic order.[111] While his and other progressive affinities for these causes dissipated among their heirs, their legacy as a matter of direct historical association with other more persistent causes remains politely overlooked—an oddly selective omission for a historical profession that has gone to extreme lengths to attach free market thinkers of the same era to a far flimsier affinity for Social Darwinism.[112]

One possible counter for classical liberals is to investigate the little-studied resistance to scientific racism, eugenicism, and similarly blameworthy causes within the works of capitalism's historical defenders. Ludwig von Mises' answer to Keynes' eugenically tinged call for the "end of laissez-faire" is particularly revealing for its sounder positioning of the contesting causes of the day: "He who rejoices that peoples are turning away from liberalism, should not forget that war and revolution, misery and unemployment for the masses, tyranny and dictatorship are not accidental companions, but are necessary results

....

111 Keynes, John Maynard. 1923. "Is Britain Overpopulated?" *New Republic*, October 31; Keynes, John Maynard. 2010. "The end of laissez-faire." *Essays in persuasion*, pp. 272-294. London: Palgrave Macmillan; Magness, Phillip W. and Hernandez, Sean J. 2017. "The Economic Eugenicism of John Maynard Keynes." *Journal of Markets and Morality*, 20(1): 79-100.

112 Hofstadter, Richard. 1944. *Social Darwinism in American thought*. Boston: Beacon Press. For a critique of Hofstadter, arguing that he overstated and misinterpreted his evidence, see Zwolinski (2015).

of the anti-liberalism that now rules the world."[113]

These examples offer just a few cases in which pronounced strains of illiberalism have emerged among the historical critics of capitalism, both left and right. They offer an avenue of research in need of further exploration as a way of contextualizing history's capitalism as it was seen and lived by persons who charged it with varying degrees of defect. Their relevance to the current state of the field is further affirmed though in the comparative inattention their own ethical shortcomings have received within a NHC literature that is simultaneously all too eager to write faults into the core of the capitalist economic system— even where historical expositors of capitalism like Smith (or later figures such as Richard Cobden, J.E. Cairnes, and Edward Atkinson) specifically assailed the very same faults.

The Future of History and Capitalism

In offering these brief remarks on the emerging and still-fluid dimensions of the history of capitalism, much more remains unanswered about the trajectory of scholarship on this topic. Research within the NHC genre has grown in appeal and acclaim within the profession, yet its foundations, as noted, have many cracks in terms of how it engages the very concept of capitalism, how it defines its terminology, and the persistent issue of inattention to complicating evidence and methods from other lines of study. Moreover, the thrust of its message does not seem to be very far removed from the anti-capitalistic biases that Hayek diagnosed half a century ago, save for a marked increase

....

113 Mises, Ludwig von. 1927. "Das Ende des Laissez-Faire, Ideen zur Verbindung von Privat und Gemeinwirtschaft." *Zeitschrift für die gesamte Staatswissenschaft.* 82: 190-91. Translation by Joseph Stromberg, https://mises.org/library/mises-keynes-1927

in the intensity of expression. In some areas such as its treatment of slavery, the NHC literature has almost unwittingly revived a strain of anti-capitalistic arguments from the late antebellum itself and adapted them to historical analysis, minus of course the embrace of slavery.

Where this leaves the classical liberal historian of capitalism is in some ways dependent upon the topic being studied in an immensely broad field. But as a general principle I will suggest taking up the role of historical interlocutor through the joint tools of economic reasoning and evidentiary empiricism. Rather than offering a broad-based theory of capitalism, replete with claims of defined systems and normative judgments of what they should or should not achieve, a scrutinizing alternative might eschew the push to define "eras" of capitalism and its antecedents entirely. Rather, we might turn our analysis to simply discerning patterns of human choice amidst conditions of scarcity, subject to what we can discern from an evidentiary basis about the values and institutional constraints surrounding a past decision.

The search for a larger systemic narrative of the past may be an unavoidable encounter. But here too the search for the larger narrative's mechanisms can also function as its own test for the specific performance of these features, and recurring patterns that might be discerned from each. As a means of inquiry, we may make no promise that capitalism will perform as an ideal system and offers no claim of inoculation against past injustices, of which there are no shortage. Instead the classical liberal historian only seeks to understand them empirically as they are examined against the causal mechanisms of human exchange, both theorized and witnessed in similar circumstances of the past.

The New History of Capitalism Has a "Whiteness" Problem

In this piece, I look at some of the backlash against criticism of the 1619 Project by its editor Nikole Hannah-Jones and by some of its historian-defenders on Twitter. A common theme of the pushback has been to focus on the race, age, and gender of the project's historian-critics, including essentially dismissing them as "old white guys." Aside from the weakness of this line of argument as a means of eschewing substantive engagement, it suffers from another problem. The contested part of the 1619 Project does not pass its own test, as the NHC literature it heavily relies upon is almost exclusively written by a small and insular group of white scholars with Ivy League connections. The NHC literature is therefore susceptible to the same charge it makes against its critics.

* * *

The *New York Times'* 1619 Project is currently undergoing a new wave of scrutiny, spurred on—curiously enough—by the political left.[114] Over the course of the last month, an obscure socialist website landed interviews with Pulitzer Prize-winning historians James McPherson and Gordon Wood, as well as noted Civil War historian James Oakes, to solicit their opinions on the *Times'* series.[115] The trio of historians pulled no punches while subjecting the project to scrutiny. Wood chastised its general thrust for diminishing the anti-slavery elements of the American Revolution, while Oakes and McPherson took issue with its reinterpretation of American capitalism as an outgrowth of plantation slavery.

Many of these observations echo my own criticisms of the project's misrepresentation of American economic history.[116] But the trio of scholars also offer significantly harsher assessments of the *Times'* initiative on the whole.

On certain narrow points this involves pressing beyond the available evidence. For example, Oakes accuses 1619 Project editor Nikole Hannah-Jones of overstating Abraham Lincoln's support for the colonization of slaves abroad (echoing a line McPherson has also used in his

....

114 Hannah-Jones, Nikole (ed). The 1619 Project *The New York Times*.

115 Mackaman, Tom. 2019. "An interview with historian James McPherson on the New York Times' 1619 Project." *World Socialist Web Site*, November 14; Mackaman, Tom. 2019. "An interview with historian Gordon Wood on the New York Times' 1619 Project." *World Socialist Web Site*, November 28; Mackaman, Tom. 2019. "An interview with historian James Oakes on the New York Times' 1619 Project." *World Socialist Web Site*, November 18.

116 Magness, Phillip W. 2019. "How the 1619 Project Rehabilitates the 'King Cotton' Thesis." *National Review*, August 26.

other works by downplaying Lincoln's commitment to this policy).[117]
This is a subject on which I possess more than a passing familiarity,
and can say with certainty that Oakes and McPherson are in error.[118]
The general criticisms from Oakes, McPherson, and Wood nonetheless
reflect substantive and thoughtful engagement with the 1619 Project's
narrative that—coming from distinguished sources—warrants a serious
response.

It is therefore dismaying, although not surprising, to see McPherson,
Wood, and Oakes being met with dismissive derision by many of the
1619 Project's defenders. "Is [Gordon Wood] under the illusion that
the [World Socialist Website is] doing anything other than using him
to club Black scholars?" asked Seth Rockman, a historian who was
consulted on the 1619 project's depiction of American capitalism.[119]

Similar comments from the history profession's younger generations
pointed out that the critics were "old white males." Other academics,
writing in this vein, accused them of excluding non-white and non-male
scholars from their assessments of the materials involved—of effectively "liv[ing] in a silo" that refuses to engage "cutting edge" work
by younger and minority scholars, as one historian put it.[120] If you've
noticed a pattern here, recall how Ana Lucia Araujo, another NHC

....

117 McPherson, James M. 2015. "Lincoln's Civil War brilliance: The real story
of the political savvy that helped end slavery." *Salon,* March 28.

118 Magness, Phillip W. and Sebastian N. Page. 2011. *Colonization After
Emancipation: Lincoln and the Movement for Black Resettlement.*

119 Rockman, Seth. 2019. "Honestly, do the socialists think GW is down with
their project?" Twitter, November 28, 2019. https://twitter.com/sethrockman/
status/1200148036208361472

120 Park, Benjamin. 2019. "Remember when McPherson couldn't name a single non-white or non-male academic historian?" Twitter, November 28, 2019.
https://twitter.com/BenjaminEPark/status/1200261304793083904

supporter, responded to me back in August 2019 when I began scrutinizing the 1619 Project's economic arguments.[121] This crowd often flees from substantive engagement over disputed scholarly claims, but they'll attack an interlocutor's race, gender, or age in a heartbeat.

Still, the neglect of a segment of the scholarly community is a potentially serious charge, even as these examples seem to service the objective of dismissing the 1619 Project's critics without actually engaging the substance of their criticisms. After all, a scholar's professional obligations include maintaining a familiarity with the latest research in his or her field when offering comments as an authority in that same field.

But is the charge even an accurate reflection of the debate over the 1619 Project?

I have to admit that I was somewhat taken aback to see this line of argument coming primarily from scholars who associate with the "New History of Capitalism" (NHC) school of thought, Rockman among them. The 1619 Project's editors relied almost entirely on NHC scholars for its treatment of slavery's economics, which appeared in a feature article by sociologist Matthew Desmond.[122] The dismissive attacks over race obscure additional fault with this editorial choice, as they set a standard that the NHC school itself does not meet.

Desmond's piece has become an acute point of contention for the project's critics, largely because he tries to weaponize the brutality of the plantation system to launch into a sweeping political attack on free

....

121 Magness, Phillip W. 2019. "How Twitter is Corrupting the History Profession." *American Institute for Economic Research,* August 29.

122 Desmond, Matthew. 2019. "American Capitalism is Brutal. You Can Trace That to the Plantation." *The New York Times*, August 14.

market capitalism in the present day. This historical claim is fraught with errors of fact and evidence, yet its anti-capitalist ideology is also a dominant theme in several key works from the NHC genre—so dominant in fact that its claimed interest in the racial dimensions of history is largely subordinate to its economic interpretation.[123]

There's also a deeper irony at play though in the NHC backlash against McPherson, Wood, Oakes, and other 1619 Project critics. Far from representing non-white scholarly voices and introducing challenges to a previously stagnant historiography of slavery, the NHC school is actually a stunning embodiment of everything it charges against its critics.

We can see how by looking at Desmond's own article. By my count, Desmond interviewed seven current academic historians when framing his piece. All seven strongly associate with the NHC school. Several of its leading figures are among the consulted voices: Ed Baptist, Sven Beckert, Walter Johnson, Calvin Schermerhorn, and Rockman, as previously mentioned. Like Desmond himself, all seven of the consulted NHC historians are also white.

By contrast, the only black voices that speak in his piece at all are long-deceased scholars such as W.E.B. Du Bois. To the extent that the article even relies on academic literature, it comes almost entirely from books by the aforementioned scholars—all of them white.

While a historian's race (or gender or age) should not be used to determine the quality of his or her work, the deployment of this form of argument against the 1619 Project's critics betrays a bizarre lack of self-awareness on the part of the NHC crowd. The modern NHC

....

123 Magness, Phillip W. 2019. "A Comment on the 'New' History of American Capitalism." *American Institute for Economic Research*, August 17.

literature on capitalism and slavery contains very few, if any, non-white voices, and Desmond's article in the 1619 project exemplifies this oversight. To borrow a little terminology from the critical theory-infused epistemology that this same school of historians often draws upon, it would appear that the New History of Capitalism has a "whiteness" problem.

The issues with the NHC complaints run deeper than its invoking of race to attack its critics though. These same scholars have made a habit of accusing their opponents of neglecting their own claimed insights to the history of slavery. That charge also runs strongly in the other direction. Despite their own self-promoted claims of "cutting edge" novelty, many of the NHC scholars actually inhabit an insular echo chamber of their own ideological compatriots.

These very same NHC scholars have attained notoriety in recent years for refusing to engage with or respond to academics in other disciplines who work on slavery, and even other historians who come from traditions outside the NHC ranks. Symptomatic of this insularity, the growing body of books and articles produced by NHC scholars often exhibit literature reviews that can only be described as ignorant or negligent of the past 50 years of scholarship on the subject, and particularly the work of economic historians.

Several academics from other branches of the slavery literature have documented this strange pattern of almost intentional disengagement from the rest of the literature by NHC historians. Economist Stanley Engerman pointed out as much in his review of the NHC genre.[124] He specifically singled out Ed Baptist, who cut off com-

....

124 Engerman, Stanley L. 2017. "Review of 'The Business of Slavery and the Rise of American Capitalism, 1815-1860' by Calvin Schermerhorn and 'The Half Has Never Been Told: Slavery and the Making of American Capitalism' by Edward E. Baptist." *Journal of Economic Literature*, 55(2): 637-43.

munications with his critics after his 2015 book *The Half Has Never Been Told* came under scrutiny by economists Alan Olmstead and Paul Rhode.[125] Baptist's silence includes a failure to correct or even address a major statistical error in his work, despite its continued repetition by other scholars and journalists.[126] As Engerman put it, Baptist's book contains "surprising omissions from the writings on slavery of the past half-century." He continues:

> Major descriptions of slave life by, for example, Kenneth Stampp (1956), Eugene Genovese (1974), and Ira Berlin (1998), are given brief (if any) mention. He does not fully engage at all in what should be of major interest to him, the last decades of works concerning economic aspects of the slave economy by scholars such as Gavin Wright (2006), Roger Ransom and Richard Sutch (1977), and Claudia Goldin (1976), not to say Robert Fogel (1989) and Fogel and Engerman (1974), whose work is both drawn upon and harshly criticized elsewhere. These have been a major analytical and statistical battleground, but are not discussed in any detail. There is only some pre-emptory discussion towards the end of the book consistent with the recent outpouring of work on slave culture and agency, issues that some now consider central to understanding the lives of those enslaved.

Glaring literature review deficiencies of this sort extend to other works in the NHC genre. The late economic historian Richard

125 Olmstead, Alan L. and Paul W. Rhode. 2018. "Cotton, slavery, and the new history of capitalism." *Explorations in Economic History*, January.

126 See chapter herein entitled "The Statistical Errors of the Reparations Agenda."

Sutch noted similar oversights in a review essay of the economic literature, particularly as it concerned the voluminous scholarly debate precipitated by Engerman and Robert Fogel's landmark 1974 study *Time on the Cross*:[127]

> Recently two historians of American slavery, Sven Beckert and Seth Rockman, dismiss their own neglect with a single sentence. "The economic history of slavery has labored in the shadows of the interpretative controversies surrounding ... *Time on the Cross*" [2016:10]. Presumably this excused them from critiquing the cliometric literature and freed them to contribute to and celebrate an alternative economic history of slavery and American economic development. Their loss (and ours) has become glaringly apparent in the recent discussion by cliometricians of what historians have come to call the "New History of Capitalism and Slavery."

In place of the necessary literature review, the NHC crowd frequently resorts to dismissiveness, derision, and ad hominem attacks. As Engerman reports, "the general response...by Baptist is to charge those who disagree with him, even when it is over what some might regard as 'merely' errors of historical fact and understanding, with racism." As the NHC backlash against more recent criticism of the 1619 Project reveals, the invoking of race for this purpose appears to be something of a default response.

This is a peculiar charge, as the main critics of the NHC literature

....

127 Sutch, Richard C. 2018. "The Economics of African American slavery: The cliometrics Debate." *NBER* working paper (number 25197), October.

make no arguments that could reasonably be described as racist. They in no way deny the violent brutality of slavery. Nor do they downplay its horrors or economic scale, asking only that such assessments remain rooted in evidence. The NHC grievance, then, appears to consist of lashing out against scholars from other schools and other disciplines who find their own arguments wanting due to issues of historical accuracy and, in some cases, unambiguous empirical errors.

In a final stroke of irony, the same group of NHC scholars recently came under fire from an older historiographical tradition on the left for appropriating and misconstruing the work of its own leading scholars. In their effort to weaponize the history of slavery against modern capitalism, many NHC scholars have wrapped themselves in the mantle of Eric Williams, a black radical from the mid-20th century Marxian tradition. His 1944 book *Capitalism and Slavery* is often invoked as a forerunner to today's NHC scholarship, though incorrectly so. Aside from the titular similarity, there's actually very little evidence that the NHC scholars engage with or meaningfully draw upon Williams' thesis. If anything, they cite it for its pairing of the words "capitalism" and "slavery" and then unintentionally invert its thesis.

Williams' most famous argument aimed to cast doubt upon conventional depictions of the abolitionist movement as a moral cause. Rather, he maintained that the rise of industrial capitalism rendered its earlier mercantile form obsolete, and with it undermined the Atlantic slave trade. The impetus for emancipation was thus a self-interested act of the capitalists, and still attached to colonial subjugation through their economic and political systems. Thus, whereas British industrial capitalism served as a self-interested agent of slavery's demise in Williams' telling, the NHC literature almost unwittingly flips the claim such that slavery becomes the mechanism of industrial capitalism's

American ascendance.

Non-NHC scholars who come from Williams' school of thought, as well as traditional Marxists in general, are none too pleased at the "new" historians' appropriation. Indeed, the *World Socialist Website*'s eagerness to host interviews with McPherson, Wood, and Oakes likely reflects the website's operators attempts to position themselves as a contesting claimant to the history of slavery on the far left. While the deterministic economic arguments of the Williams thesis have not fared well in subsequent historical evaluation, they are historiographically important and, along with his mentor C.L.R. James, form the basis of a Caribbean-centric black radical school of historical thought that is now in direct tension with the predominantly white and Ivy League-centric NHC school.[128]

Enter H. Reuben Neptune, a historian of the postcolonial Caribbean who comes from the same historiographical tradition as Williams and James. In a recent issue of the *Journal of the Early Republic,* Neptune painstakingly documents how several leading works in the NHC genre incorrectly invoke Williams as their own precursor while only engaging his text at a superficial level.[129] Beckert, Baptist, Johnson, and other NHC scholars thus end up "throwing scholarly shade" upon Williams' thesis, misrepresenting its purposes to their own ends.

Thus do we arrive at the unenviable position where scholars in the NHC genre are guilty of the very same faults that they invoke to dismiss critics of the 1619 Project. We arrive at a new historiographical

....

128 Davis, David Brion. 1988. "The Benefit of Slavery." *The New York Review of Books*, March 31.

129 Neptune, H. Reuben. 2019. "Throwin' Scholarly Shade: Eric Williams in the New Histories of Capitalism and Slaver." *Journal of the Early Republic*, 39(2): 299-326.

body of scholars that operate in their own echo chamber, that misrepresent or completely neglect scholarly works from outside of that echo chamber, and that recklessly dismiss their critics on account of a racial demography that has an even more pronounced presence in their own ranks. Furthermore, in doing so, they lay mistaken claim to a competing black radical historiographic tradition, essentially botching its most famous arguments in the process through a careless and politicized reading.

The *Times'* 1619 Project remains an evolving work, and its other contributions extend beyond the current debate over its treatment of slavery and capitalism. But notice that the project's studies of the 20th and 21st centuries have attracted far less controversy than the Desmond article or the slavery and capitalism debate.

That debate is a flashpoint for criticism precisely because of its overreliance on the flawed "New History of Capitalism" school. Until its authors and editors recognize this skew and substantively engage with the deep factual and historiographical problems that afflict this literature, they can expect to face similar criticisms from the broader scholarly world outside of the NHC genre.

What the 1619 Project's Critics Get Wrong about Lincoln

While many assessments of the 1619 Project have raised the need for significant factual corrections to its historical narrative, one area where a large number of historians go astray is its treatment of Abraham Lincoln. The 1619 Project correctly called attention to the complexities of Lincoln's own thoughts about race in a post-emancipation society, noting the tension caused by his lifelong interest in the voluntary but subsidized colonization of African-Americans abroad. Colonization makes for a lively subject of interpretive debate around Lincoln, but several prominent critics have adopted a stance that either downplays or denies the significance of this concept to Lincoln's racial beliefs.

By happenstance this aspect of Lincoln's life and presidency falls squarely in my own published research area dating back over a decade, encompassing multiple scholarly articles and a 2011 monograph on the subject. The Times' project lead Nikole Hannah-Jones even cited my work to rebut early criticisms of her treatment of Lincoln before realizing it came from a critic of other essays in the series. Nonetheless, credit is due on this specific point and, in the interest of factual accuracy, I draw upon that research to document the many ways in which other 1619 Project detractors get Lincoln wrong.

* * *

Since its publication last August, the *New York Times'* 1619 Project has come under a barrage of withering critiques. Historians took it to task for exaggerating the role of slavery as a motivating factor behind the Revolutionary War, while economists quickly dissected its empirically suspect attempt to redefine modern American capitalism as an outgrowth of the "King Cotton" plantation economies of the antebellum period.

In its worst instances, the 1619 Project amounts to an unscholarly mess of historical misrepresentations, economic fallacy, and an explicit anti-capitalist ideological agenda. To the project's further discredit, the Times' editors and main contributors have adopted a dismissive stance in response to substantive criticism, including a refusal to correct documented factual errors[130] among its historical claims.

Not all criticisms of the *Times'* initiative have hit their mark though.

Consider the case of Abraham Lincoln, whose support for the colonization of former slaves in tropical locales outside of the United States came under the scrutiny of project organizer Nikole Hannah-Jones.

....

130 See chapter herein entitled "The Case for Retracting Matthew Desmond's 1619 Project Essay."

In a speech before a group of free African Americans at the White House on August 14, 1862, Lincoln observed, "Without the institution of slavery and the colored race as a basis, the war could not have an existence." Given the likely persistence of racial conflict, he concluded, "It is better for us both, therefore, to be separated."

Hannah-Jones uses this lesser-known example of Lincoln's politics to impart complexity to his reputation as a racial egalitarian, including hints that the "Great Emancipator" exhibited misgivings over the prospect of political equality in the post-slavery United States. Several of the most effective critics of the project's faulty Revolutionary War thesis then pounced on this Civil War-era suggestion as an example of another error.

Allen Guelzo, a prominent conservative historian, dubs the characterization an "outrageous, lying slander" against Lincoln, while Sean Wilentz, a noted progressive scholar, charges that Hannah-Jones had used the issue to obscure Lincoln's larger aim of advancing emancipation, unattached to any colonization proviso.[131]

In both historians' accounts, Lincoln's interest in colonization is relegated to its limited deployment as a temporary political tool, and possibly insincerely at that, after which it could be discarded from the emancipation story.

Wilentz achieves this dismissal by erroneously reporting that Lincoln decoupled colonization from his preliminary Emancipation

....

131 Guelzo, Allen C. 2020. "The 1619 Project's outrageous, lying slander of Abe Lincoln." *New York Post*, March 3; Wilentz, Sean. 2020. "A Matter of Facts." *The Atlantic*, January 22.

Proclamation of September 1862.[132] This document's second paragraph actually announced the continuation of the government's "effort to colonize persons of African descent, with their consent." He then further excises the policy from the District of Columbia Emancipation Act, which actually contained $100,000 in colonization funding— reportedly the main factor that induced Lincoln to sign the measure.[133]

Guelzo goes even further, recasting colonization as something of a political ruse by Lincoln to lull the Northern electorate into accepting the more radical proposition of abolishing slavery. Or as he puts it, colonization was "the great tranquilizer of white anxiety" during the months leading up to the Emancipation Proclamation. Such speculations are not new. They date to the Civil War era itself, and Guelzo quotes one such example in the journalist Frederick Milnes Edge who pondered from afar that the aforementioned D.C. Emancipation Act's colonization fund had been promoted by Lincoln "to silence the weak-nerved."

Though it was unknown to Edge as he penned these words and, apparently, Guelzo today, Lincoln's own actions in the wake of the D.C. Emancipation Act contradicts this suggestion. On the day after he signed the measure, Lincoln secretly summoned the African American abolitionist and Liberian missionary Alexander Crummell to the White House for an informal conversation about soliciting recruits to use the

....

132 Wilentz, Sean. 2020. "A Matter of Facts." *The Atlantic*, January 22; Lincoln, Abraham. 1862. The first edition of Abraham Lincoln's preliminary emancipation proclamation, September 22. Available from *The Alfred Whital Stern Collection of Lincolniana.*

133 Transcription: "An Act for the Release of certain Persons held to Service or Labor in the District of Columbia." https://www.archives.gov/exhibits/featured-documents/dc-emancipation-act/transcription.html.

measure's colonization provisions.[134]

Edge's speculative explanation for Lincoln's many public colonization remarks has nonetheless proven a powerful intoxicant for historians who desire an exonerative explanation for their content. Thus writers such as Guelzo and Wilentz echo it today, and advance an account of Lincoln almost wholly divorced from his colonization arguments. With palliative deed complete and the tranquilizer serving its political purpose, Lincoln then supposedly abandoned the proposal and "sloughed off" colonization for good, to use an oft-quoted line from the diary of his secretary John Hay.

Both views are steeped in an older literature of Lincoln biography and commentary, including the two authors' own work. But as we shall see, that same literature is almost 20 years out of date, having missed several subsequent archival discoveries that belie its contentions.[135]

The first complicating factor is a succession of previously unknown records in foreign repositories revealing long-lost efforts of the Lincoln administration to secure prospective colonization sites from foreign governments.[136] With materials in the government archives of the United Kingdom, the Netherlands, Belize, Jamaica, and Denmark, these records attest to a shift in Lincoln's colonization policies that began around January 1863.

Having encountered the plagues of public graft and corruption in

....

134 Magness, Phillip W. n.d. "Lincoln to Crummell, 5/5/1862." *Phillip W. Magness*, http://philmagness.com/?page_id=407

135 Magness, Phillip W. 2014. "A brief guide to colonization documents omitted from the Collected Works of Abraham Lincoln." *Phillip W. Magness*, January 7. http://philmagness.com/?p=648

136 Magness, Phillip W. and Sebastian N. Page. 2011. *Colonization After Emancipation, Lincoln and the Movement for Black Resettlement.*

his earlier colonization ventures with private landholders, Lincoln turned to the secretive channels of diplomacy and what were seen as stable European powers with labor-starved Caribbean colonies. In sum, these State Department initiatives extend the known record of Lincoln's colonization program over a year beyond the final Emancipation Proclamation of January 1, 1863.

Second, and contrary to the suggestions of both Wilentz and Guelzo, Lincoln clearly envisioned colonization as a corollary policy to the more famous Proclamation. While Guelzo and Wilentz demarcate January 1, 1863, as the end of Lincoln's colonization interests, the 16th president actually spent the evening before his most famous act in the company of colonization negotiators. They were putting the finishing touches on a pilot program to transport some 500 freed slaves from Fort Monroe, Virginia, to a prospective colony on the Île-à-Vache off the coast of Haiti. The project's agent, Bernard Kock, returned to the White House in the company of Sen. James R. Doolittle the next day to obtain the president's signature on the finalized arrangement only an hour before he issued his more famous Proclamation.

Although the details of Kock's contract were intentionally obscured from the press so as to avoid the political corruption that plagued an earlier and more public colonization project the previous fall, Lincoln actually signaled his intention for emancipation and colonization to proceed hand-in-hand.[137] The day after the Proclamation, an anonymous editorial appeared in the Washington Morning Chronicle announcing its consummation as "initial point of separation of the black from the

137 Scheips, Paul J. 1952. "Lincoln and the Chiriqui Colonization Project." *The Journal of Negro History*, 37(4): 418-453; Lincoln, Abraham. 1862. "Annual Message to Congress." *Collected Works of Abraham Lincoln*, December 1, Vol. 5: 519-537.

white race" through voluntary colonization abroad. The article's hidden author was John Nicolay, the president's personal secretary.

Lincoln, for his own part, pitched the scheme out of a genuine concern that the post-slavery South would devolve into institutionalized racial terrorism at the hands of former plantation owners. This pessimistic appeal earned him the ire of Frederick Douglass, who denounced him as an "itinerant colonization preacher." But his scheme also resonated with other black abolitionists including Henry Highland Garnet, a leader of New York City's black community who barely escaped the violence of a white-supremacist mob during the New York Draft Riots of 1863, and John Willis Menard, who later became the first African American to win election to Congress. In fact, the 1862 White House speech highlighted in Hannah-Jones's essay entailed one such attempt to sway a free black audience into accepting colonization as a safety valve from racial oppression in a post-slavery South.

Both the Haitian venture and the arrangements with the European powers would falter over the next year, though not for want of Lincoln's own recurring efforts to breathe life into them. As the president explained to a British visitor in June 1863, colonization was his "honest desire." Lincoln nonetheless found his "colonization hobby," as he often referred to it, hamstrung by political setbacks.

William Seward, Lincoln's otherwise-loyal secretary of state, opposed the project and settled into a pattern of intentionally dragging his feet when processing the president's colonization directives.[138] At one point in August 1863, Lincoln had to personally order Seward to

....

138 Page, Sebastian N. 2017. ""A Knife Sharp Enough to Divide Us": William H. Seward, Abraham Lincoln, and Black Colonization." *Diplomatic History*, 41(2): 362-391.

transmit a signed colonization agreement to the British legation in Washington, D.C., after the secretary had sat upon it for almost two months. That same November, Seward stalled a signed colonization treaty between the United States and the Netherlands by declining to submit it to the Senate for ratification.[139]

A series of mishaps plagued the Île-à-Vache project, beginning with a smallpox outbreak shortly after the expedition set sail in April 1863 and culminating almost a year later when the colony collapsed from mismanagement and had to be rescued by the U.S. Navy. The publicity surrounding disaster and the political bickering it provoked as competing government officials rushed to point fingers of blame further dampened congressional enthusiasm for continuing the president's colonization programs.

Finally, the persistent presence of political graft caught Congress's attention during an annual review of approximately $600,000 in dedicated colonization funding in 1864. After discovering financial improprieties implicating a cabinet official and suggesting that a sitting U.S. senator had absconded with several thousand dollars from the account, legislators moved to rescind the appropriation in June 1864. This event prompted Hay's aforementioned diary entry that the president had "sloughed off" colonization, but neither Guelzo nor Wilentz supply the context of Hay's next passage:

> Mitchell says Usher allows Pomeroy to have the records of the Chiriqui matters away from the Department to cook up his fraudulent accounts by. If so, Usher ought to be hamstrung.

....

139 Douma, Michael J. 2019. *The Colonization of Freed African Americans in Suriname: Archival Sources Relating to the U.S.-Dutch Negotiations, 1860-1866.*

John Palmer Usher was the secretary of the interior, accused of permitting illicit access to the colonization account. Samuel Pomeroy was the implicated senator, having previously held a contract on a competing colonization project in modern-day Panama. Perhaps most importantly, Hay's named source for this information was James Mitchell, a longtime Lincoln associate who now served as the government's colonization commissioner.[140]

Far from signaling the abandonment of the program, Hay's passage reveals that Mitchell was whistleblowing to the White House about corruption in the program. Mitchell himself would later record a conversation with the president from the same week. Lincoln informed his colonization commissioner that the recent congressional action constituted an "unfriendly" amendment to the budget. Lincoln, it now appears, had not experienced the change of heart that Guelzo and Wilentz imply from Hay's comment. Rather, he was angry that his subordinates were stealing money from the colonization account and frustrated by Congress's decision to strip away the funding

While this setback effectively iced the remaining colonization initiatives of the administration for the duration of the Civil War, there are several signs that Lincoln intended to revive the program after the resumption of peace. After his reelection in November 1864, Lincoln moved to replace Usher in his cabinet with James Harlan, a colonization supporter and close friend of Mitchell. Lincoln also solicited his attorney general, Edward Bates, for a legal opinion that would allow him to sustain a small budget and back pay for Mitchell's office, in lieu of the suspended funding.

....

140 Page, Sebastian N. 2011. "Lincoln and Chiriqui Colonization Revisited." *American Nineteenth Century History*, 12(3): 289-325.

The final clue came on February 1, 1865, in the form of a recently discovered memorandum. Mitchell apparently met that morning with Rep. Thaddeus Stevens, the powerful chairman of the House Ways and Means Committee, to discuss a proposal that would see the colonization office's funding partially restored as the war wound to an end.[141] Stevens, who had shepherded the 13th Amendment through the House of Representatives only a day earlier, appended his signature on the memorandum for intended delivery to the president. His accompanying note read simply, "I cheerfully recommend the above named settlement."

Lincoln either never received Stevens's note, or never had the opportunity to act upon it, as he fell to an assassin's bullet on the evening of April 14, 1865. The question of what, if any, role colonization might have come to play in the racial policies of Lincoln's second term is therefore necessarily unanswerable, although Capitol Hill chatter from the early spring of 1865 hinted that Lincoln intended to appoint Mitchell to an unspecified role in the newly created Freedmen's Bureau. The former colonization commissioner's files at the National Archives contain a long list of senators' signatures on a statement endorsing this proposed transfer of roles.

What we do know for certain is how Lincoln's own friends and associates understood his position on colonization in his lifetime, as several left testimonials on the subject that chafe with the two historians' assessments. Note that Guelzo, in another critical essay on the 1619 Project, characterized the 16th president's position thusly:

....

141 Magness, Phillip W. n.d. "Thaddeus Stevens and Colonization." *Phillip W. Magness*. http://philmagness.com/?page_id=470

"Lincoln was, at best, ambivalent about colonization."[142]

Contrast this dismissive assessment with the words of William Seward, conveyed to a bedside visitor during his own long recovery from a parallel assassination attempt on the night of John Wilkes Booth's infamous deed:

> "No knife was ever sharp enough to divide us upon any question of public policy," said the Secretary, "though we frequently came to the same conclusion through different processes of thought." "Only once," he continued musingly, "did we disagree in sentiment ... His colonization scheme."

As we grapple with the substantive historical defects of the 1619 Project – and there are many – it is important to do so from a position of rigorous adherence to historical evidence. It is also important to temper our temptation to overinterpret the same evidence from the vantage point of the present. While Lincoln's colonization remarks grate the modern ear, and evince a patronizing paternalism toward the program's intended participants, they also reflect the sincerity of his anti-slavery beliefs and an accompanying recognition that white-supremacist violence would not end with the formal abolition of the institution.

This condition need not be gratuitously vilified, as the 1619 Project risks doing in the absence of temperate analysis, but nor should it be obscured with misleading and mistaken historical arguments offered for the sake of discrediting a point where the 1619 Project actually has the stronger case.

....

142 2020. "Twelve Scholars Critique the 1619 Project and the New York Times Magazine Editor Responds." *History News Network*, January 26.

Instead we might ponder why the assessments of Wilentz and Guelzo veer so far from the evidentiary record, encompassing not only new archival discoveries but also common knowledge in Lincoln's own lifetime. One eyewitness to the emancipation story left a final clue to the complexities of Lincoln's thought.

While recording his own memories after the war, Lincoln's secretary of the Navy, Gideon Welles, recounted Lincoln's simultaneous pursuit of emancipation and colonization. They "were, in his mind, indispensably and indissolubly connected."

The 1619 Project:
An Epitaph

Of the course of the 1619 Project roll-out and debate, the Times's *interactions with its scholarly critics became increasingly strained and dismissive. I experienced this rebuff directly in my efforts to prompt a correction to Matthew Desmond's essay on slavery and capitalism, but the most intense dispute involved the project's reimagining of the American Revolution as an effort to protect and preserve slavery from a posited but weakly attested British shift toward emancipation. A little over seven months after the project first appeared in print, one of its own consulted fact-checkers broke her silence and revealed that she had cautioned the paper against pushing this thesis - only to be ignored. In this essay I discuss the development, along with an intentionally understated but revealing correction that it prompted from the newspaper. When contextualized amid the larger debate, this embarrassing incident reveals the ideological nature of the 1619 Project and how the* Times'*prioritization of its political message has harmed and largely discredited its once-promising value as a work of historical interpretation.*

* * *

It took six months of heated debate to reach this point, but the *New York Times'* 1619 Project has finally offered a small but crucial concession to its critics. On March 11, the paper published an "update" to indicate that it would be changing a disputed line of text in the lead essay by Nikole Hannah-Jones.[143] The change concerns one of the more visible points of contention from the preceding months.

As originally framed, the 1619 Project depicted the preservation of slavery against a British emancipatory threat as a central motivating factor for the American Revolution. They are now relaxing that claim to suggest that preserving slavery was a motive for only *"some of* the colonists."

The *Times'* correction comes across as a minor edit on paper, but behind those two altered words is a stunning concession. Over the previous six months, Hannah-Jones maintained an unyielding hold to her original essay's claim, and did so under intense scrutiny from experts on the subject. The assignment of primacy to slavery as a revolutionary cause became a focal point of a letter by five leading historians to the *Times* calling on the paper to issue a correction, which prompted a dismissive reaction back in December from both Hannah-Jones and the magazine's editor, Jake Silverstein.[144]

Much of the contention focused upon a late 1775 attempt by Lord Dunmore, the British governor of Virginia, who moved to preserve

....

143 Silverstein, Jake. 2020. "An Update to The 1619 Project". *The New York Times*, March 11.

144 Silverstein, Jake. 2019. "We Respond to the Historians Who Critiqued The 1619 Project." *The New York Times*, December 20.

his rule by drawing the slaves of rebellious colonists into his militia in exchange for their freedom.

The Dunmore Proclamation revealed one of the many ways in which slavery cut across the other dividing lines of the revolutionary period, but it did not portend a coming general emancipation from the Crown.[145] Indeed, most slave-owning colonists perceived the measure as an attempt to incite a slave revolt against opponents of the British rule, rather than a sign of slavery's weakening position. The proclamation conveniently exempted the slaves of loyalist plantation owners, and Dunmore himself left a sordid record as supporter and beneficiary of slavery in the British colonial system. Meanwhile, as the long fight to abolish the institution made all too clear, supporters of slavery maintained firm majorities in the British Parliament at the time—and would continue in power for several decades to come.

Most of the problems with this key point in the 1619 Project's narrative appear to have stemmed from the way that Hannah-Jones went about researching and preparing her collection of essays. While the *New York Times Magazine* feature emerged under the consultation of several expert scholars in other areas of the 400-year swath of American history under its scope, it used very few specialists in the period between the American Revolution and the Civil War—arguably the most crucial period for the study of slavery in the United States.

Instead, Hannah-Jones took on this subject herself or assigned specific themes from this period to non-experts, such as Princeton sociologist Matthew Desmond who wrote an accompanying piece on the economics of slavery despite having no scholarly competencies in that subject.

....

145 See chapter herein entitled "Fact Checking the 1619 Project and Its Critics."

The results have made the period of 1775 to 1865 an acute vul-
nerability for the 1619 Project, even as the remainder of the initiative
has faced far less criticism. At this point it would be accurate to
conclude that the reputation of the project's other essays, many of
them entirely unobjectionable adaptations of scholarly insights for a
popular audience, has suffered because of the *Times'* inflexible refusal
to address erroneous historical claims in the essays by Hannah-Jones
and Desmond.

When specialists in the 1775-1865 period began to scrutinize the
Times' claims about this period, they quickly identified multiple glaring
errors of fact and interpretation alike. Hannah-Jones had grossly exaggerated the Dunmore Proclamation and misinterpreted its political
ramifications to the revolution, ahistorically recasting the British as
something of an existential threat to American slavery. In similar
fashion, Desmond botched several basic facts about the economic
history of slavery.[146] He severely overstated the economic significance
of cotton to industrialization, while also misreading and misrepresenting evidence he enlisted to argue that the plantation economy
stains and discredits modern American capitalism.[147]

While the *Times* has thus far evaded scrutiny of Desmond's claims,
Hannah-Jones began casting about after the fact for scholars who would
lend credence to her elevation of slavery to preeminence among the
motives behind the Declaration of Independence.

In time she was able to cherry-pick an eclectic literature from

....

146 See chapter herein entitled "How the 1619 Project Rehabilitates the 'King
Cotton' Thesis."

147 See chapter herein entitled "The Case for Retracting Matthew Desmond's
1619 Project Essay."

a handful of historians that assign more emphasis to the effects of Dunmore's act on the revolutionary cause. However, as Cathy Young documents, most of these scholars assert much more tempered variants of this thesis under heavy qualifiers that were absent from Hannah-Jones's own depiction, and the few who do not offer arguments that collapse under evidentiary scrutiny.[148]

At the same time, Hannah-Jones's own response to her scholarly critics devolved from an initial respectful engagement to aggressive derision. She attacked the scholarly credentials of James McPherson and Gordon Wood, two of the most famous historians to question her narrative.[149] In one perplexing tweet, she singled out the critics as "white historians" (oddly neglecting the lack of racial diversity among the scholars who advised Desmond's own 1619 Project contribution).[150] When a group of conservative African-American academics and journalists launched a competing "1776 Project" in early 2020 to offer a counter-narrative, Hannah-Jones bombarded them with a string of personal attacks, the gist of which amounted to declaring

....

148 Young, Cathy. 2020. "The Fight Over the 1619 Project." The Bulwark, February 9, 2020.

149 Hannah-Jones, Nikole. 2019. "And this dude is defending that shit, actually arguing we should take this "preeminent" scholar seriously." Twitter, November 22, 2019. https://twitter.com/nhannahjones/status/1197762958039932928; Hannah-Jones, Nikole. 2019. "Who considers him preeminent? I don't." Twitter, November 22, 2019. https://twitter.com/nhannahjones/status/1197764022550122496

150 Hannah-Jones, Nikole. 2019. "LOL. Right, because white historians have produced truly objective history." Twitter, November 21, 2019. https://twitter.com/nhannahjones/status/1197573220037201922; see chapter herein entitled "The New History of Capitalism Has a "Whiteness" Problem."

them unworthy of her attention.[151]

From Silverstein's rebuff of the essay's historian critics to Hannah-Jones's dismissive and insulting demeanor, the message was clear.[152] The *Times* would not be amending its content, even to account for substantive evidence-based criticism of its factual and interpretive mistakes. This inflexible stance even extended to clearly documented errors, such as Hannah-Jones's misuse of the Dunmore proclamation. When I directed Silverstein to a line in Desmond's essay that specifically contradicted its own cited source by imparting a slavery-based origin story to modern Microsoft Excel spreadsheets, he similarly declined to offer any correction or clarification.[153] The paper's commitment to its published claims remained inflexible, no matter the error. Scholarly assessments of the project itself were unwelcome, unless they offered support to the 1619 Project's preexisting narrative.

So what brought about the *Times'* sudden, if underplayed, reversal?

On March 6, 2020, *Politico* published a surprise essay by historian Leslie M. Harris that upended the 1619 Project debate.[154] Although its author chided some of the historian-critics of the project for allegedly understating slavery in their own work, she also had a stunning

....

151 2020. "1776 Project." *1776 Unites*; Rosen, Christine. 2020. "The 'Beyonce of Journalism' and Her Critics." *Commentary Magazine*, February 18; Hemingway, Mark. 2020. "The New York Times Goes All In on Flawed 1619 Project." *Real Clear Politics*, February 21.

152 See chapter herein entitled "The Statistical Errors of the Reparations Agenda."

153 Murray, J., Olmstead, A., Logan, T., Pritchett, J., & Rousseau, P. 2015. "Roundtable of Reviews for 'The Half Has Never Been Told: Slavery and the Making of American Capitalism' By Edward E. Baptist." *The Journal of Economic History,* 75(03): 919-931.

154 Harris, Leslie M. 2020. "I Helped Fact-Check the 1619 Project. The Times Ignored Me." *Politico*, March 6.

revelation about Hannah-Jones's essay.

The previous summer Harris had been contacted by the *Times* to serve as a fact-checker on the 1619 Project's discussions of slavery, one of her areas of specialization. The newspaper had asked her to verify the following claim:

> One critical reason that the colonists declared their independence from Britain was because they wanted to protect the institution of slavery in the colonies, which had produced tremendous wealth. At the time there were growing calls to abolish slavery throughout the British Empire, which would have badly damaged the economies of colonies in both North and South.

In Harris's own words, "I vigorously disputed the claim. Although slavery was certainly an issue in the American Revolution, the protection of slavery was not one of the main reasons the 13 Colonies went to war." The *Times'* editors ignored her warning and ran with Hannah-Jones's argument anyway.

It took less than a week for the *Times* to migrate from its previous steadfast defense of the claim to the concession noted at the outset of this essay. Even then, the concession remains understated.

The newspaper's peculiar wording attempted to chalk the confusion up to interpretive ambiguities by its readers. In Silverstein's words, the *Times* recognized "that our original language could be read to suggest that protecting slavery was a primary motivation for all of the colonists. The passage has been changed to make clear that this was a primary motivation for some of the colonists."

Contrast that with the original passage, which stated, "Conveniently left out of our Founding mythology is the fact that one of the primary reasons the colonists decided to declare their independence from Britain was because they wanted to protect the institution of slavery."

There is no issue where the passage "could be read to suggest" an erroneous historical claim. It made that claim outright in unambiguous language that Hannah-Jones subsequently doubled down upon and, until the correction, showed few signs of ever relaxing or qualifying.

Still, the concession revealed more than its guarded conciliatory language displayed. Although they are conspicuously unacknowledged in Silverstein's correction note, the critics of the 1619 Project were on solid ground to question this claim and did so when it first appeared in print over six months earlier. The *Times*, in turn, behaved atrociously in deflecting and denying a substantive scholarly challenge to its content until its hand was forced.

Thus we are left with "could be read to suggest." That tepid backtracking, in effect, gave away the game. It's a fitting epitaph to what could have been an important and provocative contribution to historical inquiry about the lasting harms of slavery in the United States, but instead veered down the path of an ideological project, consumed by maintaining its own 21st-century political narrative above the history it weaponized to that cause.

About the Author

Phillip W. Magness is an economic historian specializing in the 19th century United States. He is the author of numerous works on the political and economic dimensions of slavery, the history of taxation, and the history of economic thought.

About AIER

The American Institute for Economic Research in Great Barrington, Massachusetts, was founded in 1933 as the first independent voice for sound economics in the United States. Today it publishes ongoing research, hosts educational programs, publishes books, sponsors interns and scholars, and is home to the world-renowned Bastiat Society and the highly respected Sound Money Project. The American Institute for Economic Research is a 501c3 public charity.

Index

1619 Project. *See also* Desmond, Matthew; Hannah-Jones, Nikole
  contributions of, 111
  messaging of, 1–2, 29, 131–32
  remediable faults of, 56
  response to criticism, 2, 12, 37–39, 54–55, 66, 114
  scholarly guidance on, 37, 52–54, 66, 111, 127, 130–31
1619 Project, discourse on
  in general, 4, 29, 37–39, 114
  American Revolution, 39–45, 125–32
  capitalism, 50–52
  Lincoln, 45–49
1776 Project, 129–30

A
abolitionists, 23–29, 90. *See also* emancipation movement
accounting errors, 10, 18, 31–36, 81
accounting practices, 18, 58–60, 130
activism, 1–2, 4. See also ideological advocacy
American Revolution, slavery in, 37, 39–45, 125–29, 131–32
Anderson, Carol, 34–35
anti-capitalist mentality
  contemporary, 3–4, 28–29, 36, 50, 71–72, 77, 85–87, 90, 99–100, 104–5
  diagnosis of, 4, 69–71, 99
  pre-20th-century, 90–94
  progressive-era, 94–98
Araujo, Ana Lucia, 103–4
Arthur Tappan & Co., 24–27

B
Bahamas, 42
Baptist, Ed
  calibrated-torture thesis, 10–12, 63–65
  capitalism's stain, 9–10
  scholarly practices, 10–13, 18, 106–8
  slavery's economic share, 10, 18, 31–34, 79–81
Baradara, Mehrsa, 53–54
Bates, Edward, 121
Beckert, Sven, 9, 60, 79, 87–88, 93, 108
biological innovations, 11, 62–64
black radicals, 109–11
boycotts, 24, 26
Bynum, Victoria, 38, 44–45, 50, 52

Made in the USA
San Bernardino, CA
10 June 2020